Isak Dinesen's AFRICA

Images of the Wild Continent
from the Writer's Life and Words

*With text chosen from the memoirs and letters
of Isak Dinesen
and photographs by Yann Arthus-Bertrand,
Peter Beard, Frank Connor, David C. Fritts,
Douglas Kirkland, Galen Rowell, Günter Ziesler
and other contributors*

Introduction by Judith Thurman

SIERRA CLUB BOOKS
SAN FRANCISCO

The Sierra Club, founded in 1892 by John Muir, has devoted itself to the study and protection of the earth's scenic and ecological resources—mountains, wetlands, woodlands, wild shores and rivers, deserts and plains. The publishing program of the Sierra Club offers books to the public as a nonprofit educational service in the hope that they may enlarge the public's understanding of the Club's basic concerns. The point of view expressed in each book, however, does not necessarily represent that of the Club. The Sierra Club has some sixty chapters coast to coast, and in Canada, Hawaii, and Alaska. For information about how you may participate in its programs to preserve wilderness and the quality of life, please address inquiries to Sierra Club, 730 Polk Street, San Francisco, California 94109.

LIBRARY OF CONGRESS CATALOGING IN PUBLICATION DATA
Dinesen, Isak, 1885–1962.
    Isak Dinesen's Africa.

    Bibliography: p. 140
    Includes index.
    1. Kenya—Description and travel—Views.   2. Dinesen,
Isak, 1885–1962—Homes and haunts—Kenya.   3. Kenya—
Social life and customs—1895–1963.   4. Country life—
Kenya.   I. Title.
DT433.524.D56   1985   967.6'203   85-8366
ISBN 0-87156-821-7

Jacket and book design by Paula Schlosser
Printed by Dai Nippon Printing Company, Ltd., Tokyo, Japan
Map by Earth Surface Graphics

10   9   8   7   6   5   4   3   2   1

[CONTENTS]

If I know a song of Africa . . . of the Giraffe, and the African new
moon lying on her back, of the ploughs in the fields, and the
sweaty faces of the coffee-pickers, does Africa know a song of me?
Would the air over the plain quiver with a colour that I had had on,
or the children invent a game in which my name was, or the full
moon throw a shadow over the gravel of the drive that was like me,
or would the eagles of Ngong look out for me?

From *Out of Africa*

[PREFACE]

IN HIS INTRODUCTION to *The Life and Destiny of Isak Dinesen*, an annotated collection of black-and-white photographs from the Dinesen archive, editor Frans Lasson notes that

she refused to accompany the description of her African life with photographs, despite the fact that innumerable books of travel were then being photographically illustrated. . . . Her book had no need for pictures, seen through the lens of a mechanical receiver. Each vision in *Out of Africa* was rooted in a deeper reality than the photographical; each was interpreted through the eyes of an artist and etched by the passion of a poet.

That *Out of Africa*, or any classic literary work, requires no visual embellishment ought to be self-evident. At least on the surface, then, it may seem presumptuous for a publisher to compile a book of Isak Dinesen's writings about Africa "illustrated" with photographs. If so, it is presumption with a sound precedent, for *Isak Dinesen's Africa* is very much in the tradition of some notable Sierra Club books of the past that have mated the words of great writers, describing some of the world's special places, with fine photographic images of those places. Examples in this genre include *In Wildness Is the Preservation of the World*, with photographs by Eliot Porter matched to passages from Thoreau, and *Not Man Apart*, with text by Robinson Jeffers and photographs of the Big Sur coast by several contributors, including Ansel Adams and Edward Weston. More recently, *Alaska: Images of the Country* set portions of John McPhee's *Coming Into the Country* alongside the work of Galen Rowell.

These volumes are not the sort of illustrated travel books that Dinesen rightly shunned in preserving the integrity of her own vision of Africa. In the kind of pictorial book represented by the above titles and, we

hope, by the present one, photographs complement words *without* strictly illustrating them. Rather than attempting to depict the exact content of a text passage, they attempt to evoke a mood, an ambiance, or a theme suggested by the words.

This oblique, nonliteral approach to the blending of text and photographs can be seen, without stretching a point too much, as parallel with Dinesen's approach to her memoirs about Africa. Her task as a literary artist was not to take the reader on a guided tour of Kenya in the 1920s—though she wrote many precise and informed descriptions of locales—nor even to give a strict account of her eighteen-year existence there. Scholars have demonstrated the extent to which *Out of Africa* and *Shadows on the Grass* depart from or transmute reality by comparing them with Dinesen's letters and with accounts by her contemporaries. In composing her memoirs, motives both personal and literary led her to distill from her material an Africa of the mind—an image of Africa formed through the lens of her own experience and aims.

Similarly, our aim has been to create pictorial books that transmit the experience of place in all ways that photography is capable of, which range well beyond simple documentation. Generally there is an informational component, but nearly always the content is shaped by the photographer's vision, so that what strikes the viewer about a particular scene or subject may be primarily a quality of light, a dominance of form, a field of color, a dynamic sense of movement, a pattern of detail or texture—or any of countless convergences of subject with the photographer's eye.

Because many photographers are represented in this book, the perspective shifts frequently. This seems appropriate, given the immense canvas of Africa on which Dinesen draws as a writer, and the distinctive, rigorously stylized voice of the writings themselves. That voice will permit no sustained competition from the personal vision of another artist, and almost surely no one photographer has yet made a quest out of tracing Dinesen's literary path across Africa. The editor's task here was to find photographic images, from many sources, that speak to the content of the selected prose passages—in some cases as a literal echo, as with pictures of specific animals and landforms, or with the black-and-white historical photos. In other cases the images are representative of a kind of landscape Dinesen portrays (all the photographs were taken in Kenya and Tanzania, though not necessarily in the exact places described in the accompanying text). Or they may be expressive of a time of day, a condition of weather, a visual perspective, a human characteristic, or a mood. Occasionally a photograph recreates an event in the author's life; in this category are a group of photographs supplied by Universal Pictures from the location shooting of the motion picture "Out of Africa."

If these images from the film, which appear to have been created in Karen Blixen's own era, seem to sit comfortably on the page with photographs of Africa from the recent past, it is because the overall aim in selecting pictures was to render a portrait of a timeless Africa, in much the way that Dinesen's written portrait seems to stand outside time. To the same end —and to allow Dinesen's words to serve as sole commentary on the images—captions do not accompany the photographs, which are identified and credited at the end of the book.

The excerpts from the work of Isak Dinesen that appear here are taken from three sources. The majority come from *Out of Africa*, probably Dinesen's best-known book and possibly the most widely read description of Africa ever written. First published in 1937, it is among those rare books that can change the life of its reader: a dramatic example is the photographer Peter Beard, who, after reading it as a very young man, set off on a pilgrimage to Kenya, and then sought out the elderly and reclusive author at her Danish home, Rungstedlund. He has produced three extraordinary books set in Dinesen's East African venues (including one based on the recollections of her former servant, Kamante), and lives today on land that was once part of Karen Blixen's coffee plantation. Certainly *Out of Africa* was the primary wellspring for this

book—nowhere else in literature is the power and allure of the African landscape conveyed in such visually evocative prose. Part of its great strength as literary art lies in the tension between a participant's involvement —her fiercely acute observation of the fine grain of daily life—and an artist's detachment, which allowed her to arrange the disparate elements of memoir into a harmonious pattern. Her biographer, Judith Thurman, characterizes the terrain of *Out of Africa* as "a landscape [seen] from the air."

Shadows on the Grass is Dinesen's second Africa memoir, published in 1960 and, in Thurman's words, "embroidering on the austere canvas of *Out of Africa*." Selections from its seven interlinked stories are also included here, as are excerpts from Dinesen's remarkable *Letters from Africa 1914–1931*, which did not appear until 1981. Unlike the memoirs, which were written in English, Dinesen's published letters were translated from the original Danish, and convey her experience of Africa with greater immediacy (and in some instances greater accuracy) than the carefully distilled memoirs. Excerpts from the letters are headed by the name of the recipient and can be so identified here; the underlining of certain words and phrases in the letters indicates where Dinesen used an English expression in the original (as distinct from her use of italics for emphasis). The note on sources at the end of this book indicates which of the remaining excerpts come from *Out of Africa* and which from *Shadows on the Grass*.

The text passages were chosen, from this rich reservoir of words, on the basis of several criteria: for qualities that invited a visual complement, for their own power of sensory evocation, and also, in sum, to build up a picture of Isak Dinesen's life and occupations in Africa. The passages are grouped into sections that roughly parallel the course of her sojourn in the Kenya highlands, or that express dominant themes of her existence there—for example, her intense and complicated feelings for the Africans, or her enthusiasm for going off on safari. Each section is prefaced by a brief biographical note. We hope that readers who are relatively new to Dinesen's life and work (or at least its African phase) may find incentive here to explore this writer's fascinating career further, and that already devoted readers of Dinesen may derive a deeper understanding of her African experience, which was so important in shaping that career.

Nowadays great sportsmen hunt with cameras. The practice started while I was still in Africa; Denys [Finch Hatton] as a white hunter took out millionaires from many countries, and they brought back magnificent pictures, the which however to my mind (because I do not see eye to eye with the camera) bore less real likeness to their object than the chalk portraits drawn up on the kitchen door by our Native porters. It is a more refined sport than shooting, and provided you can make the lion join into the spirit of it you may here, at the end of a pleasant, platonic affair, without bloodshed on either side, blow one another a kiss and part like civilized beings. I have no real knowledge of the art; I was a fairly good shot with a rifle, but I cannot photograph.

This passage from *Shadows on the Grass* raises issues beyond Isak Dinesen's lack of enthusiasm for game photography, of which Judith Thurman observes, "It was not a matter of life and death, and therefore it held no interest for her." It is difficult for many contemporary readers, especially if they are committed environmentalists, to reconcile Karen Blixen's evident passion for and deep sensitivity to the wild lands and wild creatures of Africa with the urge to hunt big game for sport, which she shared wholeheartedly with most of her contemporaries in Kenya. We know, from our present vantage, that the decimation of Africa's great animal populations is traceable directly to the uncontrolled sport-hunting engaged in by early colonists, their safari clients, and thousands who followed, and to the international trade in skins, furs, and horn, both in conjunction with environmental pressures such as drought and habitat loss due to development. Without coming to grips with the moral and spiritual issues that surround hunting in general, or with Dinesen's personal assertion that shooting big game was "a fine and fascinating art" or even "a love-affair . . . with the game," we can still recognize that she and her contemporaries lived in a different world from ours. Their Africa must indeed have seemed like an unspoiled Eden whose natural bounty could never be seriously compromised by the handful of white settlers then scattered throughout its vastness. Lacking the benefit of hindsight and any sense of ecological consequences, they repeated the error that people from developed societies have committed on wilderness frontiers around the planet, with similarly predictable results.

In trying to make a book that looks timeless, that gives some sense of how wild Africa might have looked in Karen Blixen's day, we cannot ignore the changes, mostly destructive ones, that time has brought to the East African landscape. There are hints here and there in Dinesen's work that she herself may have foreseen some of these changes; very early in *Out of Africa* she writes, "When the Colony prospers and Nairobi, the capital, grows into a big city, the Ngong Hills might have made a matchless game park for it. But during my last years in Africa many young Nairobi shop-people ran out into the hills on Sundays, on their motor-cycles, and shot at anything they saw, and I believe that the big game will have wandered away from the hills, through the thorn-thickets and the stony ground further South."

Knowing what we do about Dinesen's affinity for the outdoor life, for wildness expressed in human and nonhuman nature, for the aesthetic and spiritual wealth embodied in an untrammeled landscape, we can guess with some confidence what her feelings would have been about the urgent conservation problems facing Africa today—however romantically or impractically she might have declared those feelings. If Isak Dinesen's Africa exists today chiefly through her words and through images captured on film, there exists also a real, changing, troubled, yet still magical Africa to be cherished, safeguarded, and reclaimed.

Observing Karen Blixen at work on a manuscript, her African servant Kamante, one of *Out of Africa*'s memorable figures, shows her a copy of *The Odyssey* and admonishes her,

"Look, Msabu . . . this is a good book. It hangs together from the one end to the other. Even if you hold it up and shake it strongly, it does not come to pieces. The man who has written it is very clever. But what you write," he went on, with both scorn and with a sort of friendly compassion, "is some here and some there. When the people forget to close the door it blows about, even down on the floor and you are angry. It will not be a good book."

The book at hand has often, in the course of its compilation, seemed to be "some here and some there." Whether it is a good book is for others to decide; that it exists at all is due to the efforts and good will of many people. The editor wishes to thank, first, Esther Margolis, whose creative publishing sense was the catalyst for a Sierra Club book of Africa photographs and the words of Isak Dinesen, and whose advice and counsel were instrumental at all stages from concept to finished book. This book could not have been created without the cooperation and support of Universal City Studios, Inc., particularly that of Sydney Pollack, who produced and directed the motion picture production "Out of Africa"; Michele Reese and Marvin Antonowsky of Universal Pictures Marketing; Frank Rodriguez, Universal's conscientious and helpful photo editor; and the talented photographers Douglas Kirkland and Frank Connor, who shot photographs for this book in the course of documenting the filming of "Out of Africa."

For permission to reprint excerpts from the copyrighted works of Isak Dinesen used in this book, we are grateful to the Rungstedlund Foundation and to Dinesen's publishers, Random House and the University of Chicago Press. Florence Feiler, U.S. representative of the Rungstedlund Foundation, provided generous assistance in clearing permissions and obtaining many of the archival photographs reproduced here.

Special thanks are due to Judith Thurman, whose award-winning biography *Isak Dinesen: The Life of a Storyteller*, was both an inspiration and a constantly thumbed reference in the making of this volume, and who consented to re-immerse herself in Dinesen's life and work in order to write the illuminating introduction that appears here.

Sierra Club Books has frequent occasion for gratitude to the gifted photographers who contribute to our publications, and never more so than with this project. Many photographers and stock agencies with whom we have worked in the past responded to our request for material, providing an exceptionally rich and varied collection of images. Space does not permit individual acknowledgment of all the photographic contributors here, but they are named in the section of photo credits at the end. An exception must be made in the case of Peter Beard, who made available not only some of his own remarkable photographs of African wildlife but also his personal collection of archival photographs from Karen Blixen's era and of the Ngong farm in later years.

Book designer Paula Schlosser gracefully transformed an editorial conception into a clean and stylish display of text and visuals, and her enthusiasm for the project made the design process unusually rewarding. The text was set in type by Mackenzie-Harris Corporation of San Francisco, and Dai Nippon Printing Company of Tokyo gave us photo reproduction of their usual superb quality under scheduling pressures that might have caused another printer to cut corners.

Finally, I must thank my colleagues at Sierra Club Books for their understanding of and professional dedication to this project, and their tolerance of the editor's obsessive tendencies during its emergence. In particular, thanks to Frances Spear, who provided indispensible follow-up in many phases of the work; Eileen Max and Susan Ristow of our production staff, who took on a huge task in difficult circumstances, manipulated schedules in ways never before conceived, and made a book that "hangs together from one end to the other"; and publisher Jon Beckmann, whose sage and cautionary guidance, and above all, whose confidence and trust in the editor, are immeasurably appreciated.

Diana Landau
Executive Editor
Sierra Club Books

[INTRODUCTION]

The Hand of Distance
by Judith Thurman

"... to the South-West, I saw the Ngong Hills. The noble wave of the mountain rose above the surrounding flat land, all air-blue. But it was so far away that the four peaks looked trifling, hardly distinguishable, and different from the way they looked from the farm. The outline of the mountain was slowly smoothed and levelled out by the hand of distance."

From *Out of Africa*

ISAK DINESEN LEFT Africa in 1931, never to return. For a while she kept in touch with her servants and a few of her old friends, but one after another they disappeared—Africa has a habit of absorbing people "into its mould." Then the war came; her health declined; both the rigors of a return journey and her fear that it might be an anticlimax deterred her. This left an unclosed parenthesis in an otherwise remarkably shapely life.

In the early thirties, however, Isak Dinesen had cherished a scheme for "building a bridge" to Africa—a hospital for Masai children that she hoped to endow with the royalties from *Seven Gothic Tales*. Albert Schweitzer, whom she sought out for advice, strongly discouraged her. He was moved by her idealism but shocked by her frailty, and also somewhat amused by her underestimate of the expense.

Grand but impractical ideas were typical of Isak Dinesen. So was her fondness for fragile idealists, out of place in a disillusioned world. Charles Bulpett, Baron von Brackel, Miss Malin Nat-og-Dag—they are gallant in their manners, extravagant in their fantasies, but ruined in their real lives. The dreamer, Dinesen tells us, is someone who has been planted in life like a coffee tree with a bent taproot. "That tree will never thrive, nor bear fruit, but it will flower more richly than the others."

A bent taproot produces a great and perhaps excessive flowering of character—at the expense of wholeness.

That was how Isak Dinesen experienced her own predicament in 1935, when she sat down to write *Out of Africa*, and to make a reckoning with her losses. She was fifty, and her "real life" was behind her. So was her health: she was suffering from tertiary syphilis of the spine, contracted in 1913 from her husband. The people she had loved most, her real intimates, were all dead.[*] Having spent eighteen years in a feudal country, she was a stranger in socialist Denmark, particularly in its literary circles—an unwelcome relic of the *ancien régime*. And having lost the scope, freedom, and eventfulness of her life in Africa, she was once again a child in her mother's house. This was probably the deepest point of her fall.

Rungstedlund was the model for all the chaste and gloomy "parsonages" of her tales. They are places of genteel confinement for children who feel like changelings in their own milieux: pagans misplaced among the

---

[*] Her father, Wilhelm, a suicide in 1895; her first love, Hans Blixen (her husband Bror's twin brother), in a plane crash in 1918; her best friend and cousin (Wilhelm's niece), Daisy Frijs, a suicide the same year; Denys Finch Hatton, her lover and "living ideal," in a plane crash in 1931. The casualty list has a strange, incestuous rhyme scheme.

A strangely shaped cloud over the Ngong Hills.
BY THOMAS DINESEN/COURTESY OF THE RUNGSTEDLUND FOUNDATION.

timid and God-fearing. Like her heroine Alkmene, or the fawn, Lulu, the young Tanne Dinesen had always plotted to escape from her well-meaning captors, but had discovered she was hobbled by her own gratitude to them. Rungstedlund had made her homesick for the African highlands and what they stood for—"a vital assurance and lightness of heart"—long before she had ever heard of them.

Every dreamer knows that it is entirely possible to be homesick for a place you have never been to, perhaps more homesick than for familiar ground. When you see your "paradise" for the first time, its rightness surprises you. The face of an imaginary friend, coming to life, might strike a daydreaming child in the same way. Dinesen puts it succinctly in *Out of Africa*: "You woke up in the morning and thought, 'Here I am, where I ought to be.'"

That sense of home came from her father, who would certainly have found his own element in the highlands. Wilhelm Dinesen was an immensely restless, vital man. His character and tastes were patrician —"love, war and the hunt"—but his politics were liberal, and he was the black sheep of a reactionary family. At twenty-five he had left Denmark to fight the Franco-Prussian War on the French side. After their defeat, the fall of the Paris Commune, and the death of a young woman he had loved—all in the same spring—he sailed for America to spend a year in the wilderness. The gesture and pilgrimage were typically romantic, the latter a search for peace through the trials of hardship and solitude, and for connection with animals and nature. Even then, however, the wilderness was under siege. Wilhelm was an unusually lucid and bitter critic of the process by which the American government was exterminating the Indians to steal their land. "They sometimes find it necessary to decimate [them] with the help of soldiers," he wrote, "though liquor, smallpox, venereal disease and other maladies usually do the trick, in concert with the extermination of their vital necessity—game. . . . In a short time they sell their land to the government in exchange for a Reservation, a miserable little tract which they cannot leave without permission of an agent. Here, for a few years, they lead an abominable existence until . . . the whites get tired of having these wretched beggars in their backyard and send them further west. . . ." More than sympathy, Dinesen felt a deep affinity for the Indians he had lived among, for their integrity and their doom. His daughter would be proud to feel she enjoyed a similar relation with the Africans.

"Tanne," as the family called her, was her father's favorite child: his confidante; the heir to his talent, charisma, and instability. She gives a sketch of their relationship in her tale "Alkmene": "[Its] chief feature was a deep, silent understanding of which the others could not know. We seemed, both of us, to be aware that we were like one another in a world different from us."

That sense of a secret covenant with her father, of having been the chosen one, was the decisive privilege of her life. While he was alive, Wilhelm rescued Tanne from the gloom of the "parsonage" and took her for long walks through the woods or by the Sound. He educated her senses; taught her to distinguish grasses, trees, and the tracks of animals. He willed her his love of nature and his conviction that bourgeois life was its betrayer.

Dinesen would find an echo of her father in all the daredevils, poets, and fallen angels of Romantic literature. Their transgressions helped to balance the example set by the women in her life, which was of others." But she also understood what the price of erotic freedom was in a developed world. It was the fate of the tree with the bent taproot.

Wilhelm Dinesen killed himself when his daughter was ten. His son, Thomas, believed that he did so because he had discovered he was suffering from syphilis, and couldn't bear the thought, after such a vigorous life, of the physical degeneration—or the shame, after setting such store in honor, for his family and to his name. Isak Dinesen couldn't help but take his death as a desertion, and she would never recover from an "irrational terror of . . . abandoning one's life and soul to something one [could] lose again."

But if she held him responsible for her neediness, Wilhelm remained a hero to her. There would always be, in her thinking and in her taste for and judgment of people, a threshold separating the wild from the domestic, the "decent" from the "respectable," those who would, given the choice, always prefer the unreasonable risks of the lion hunt to the rational satisfactions of family life. "Come now," she said to her lover, Denys Finch Hatton, on a birthday, when he was feeling that life didn't have much point. "Let us go and risk our entirely worthless lives . . . *frei lebt wer sterben kann.*"*

Baron Bror Blixen in his study, 1917.
COURTESY OF THE RUNGSTEDLUND FOUNDATION.

Karen Blixen and Thomas Dinesen in the garden of the farm, 1922.
COURTESY OF THE RUNGSTEDLUND FOUNDATION.

Finding it difficult to work on *Out of Africa* at Rungstedlund, Isak Dinesen packed her books into her old car and drove as far north in Denmark as she could go —to Skagen, at the tip of Jutland, where the Baltic crashes into the North Sea. This is a flat, windswept landscape of grey sky and shifting sand dunes: a place as remote as you could imagine from the Ngong Hills.

Winter, at such a latitude, gives you the leisure, but also the need to mull. Poetry, music, and abstract thought make up for the deprivation of the senses. In Africa, they are kept continuously *intelligent*: charged by all those timeless fears and pleasures that civilization has done its best to make obsolete. When survival becomes gainful employment, it is almost impossible to be bored or depressed. The real wilderness has, for that reason, always attracted a certain kind of rugged drifter.

The Europeans who emigrated to the East African highlands in the teens of the century tended to fall into the rugged-drifter category. They also had something in common with the aristocrats of Boccacio's *De-*

cameron, fleeing the plague in Florence to a villa in the pure air of the hills, where they told stories to keep death at bay. The emigrants' plagues were convention, anxiety, and the pressures to succeed, breed, or conform to a certain mold. Some of them were nostalgic for the unlimited feudal power that their families had once wielded. Others were seeking a clean sense of identity or place. They fell greedily upon this vast, "pure" country that was almost impossible to resist calling Paradise.

It is the music of a place that gives the impression of its purity: the finely balanced music of many strings, equal in tension. But it is also a relatively simple matter to untune them. The emigrants did so with paved roads, shooting for sport, and racial contempt. They did so with a hut tax that obliged the Africans to work on the white farms and with an alien notion of authority: there were no "Paramount Chiefs" among the Kikuyus until the British decided they would be an administrative convenience.

But the most alienating and disruptive import was the Western concept of possession, of inheritance—which begins at the moment of dispossession, of disinheritance, as it did in the original Eden. The real loss of innocence is the realization that something you have never thought to lack has been stolen from you. How you value *yourself* in a fallen world always refers, thereafter, to that sense of loss. It has to do with your relative power or helplessness to console yourself with a supply of *things*—symbols of wholeness.

It is strange, when you think about it, that an unhappy young woman, raised in a northern country, rich from the clever deals that her grandfather made in the commodities markets of Europe, could console herself to the tune of 6,000 acres of African earth, hills, streams, forest, and game.

Ingeborg Dinesen with the tame owl, Minerva, on the farm, 1925.
BY THOMAS DINESEN/COURTESY OF THE RUNGSTEDLUND FOUNDATION.

Juma, Kamante, and others with Karen Blixen's dogs in front of the shambas.
BY THOMAS DINESEN/COURTESY OF THE RUNGSTEDLUND FOUNDATION.

The injustice of her inherited wealth did not stop Isak Dinesen from loving "her" coffee, "her" buffalo and lion, and her feudal role. Nor did it stop her from feeling, as her friend Ingrid Lindstrom put it, "an idiotic reverence" for the aristocracy. Their sense of boundless entitlement was so alluring to her, I think, precisely because her own insecurity was, as she herself put it, so "pathological." But unlike most of her contemporaries, Dinesen was keenly aware of her presumption in laying claim to a part of Africa. She assesses her own possessiveness with a complex irony, leeches it of nostalgia. That firmness is partly what makes *Out of Africa* such a useful parable about loss, and such a moving personal story.

Admirers of Isak Dinesen often ask me if I think she would have become a writer had she stayed in Africa. It would be presumptuous to say: every fate has many forks to it. She would probably not have written a memoir with the same historical and mythic depth of field. She needed to lose her subject in order to see it whole.

But Dinesen had already done a great deal of writing before the farm was sold. Among her papers was an essay on love and marriage, which takes an eighteenth-century view of the institution—that it should be entered into as a shared ideal rather than a romantic passion. She had drafted a few tales that read like swatches for her mature work, and perhaps she

Kinanjui, chief of the Kikuyu living on the farm, attends a ngoma, *1925.*
COURTESY OF THE RUNGSTEDLUND FOUNDATION.

[xv]

would have cut and finished them. And she had written hundreds of letters home, mostly to her mother, which are wonderful to read. Their voice is unguarded —not transcendent and serene, like the narrator's voice in *Out of Africa*. It is the voice of a young woman still in conflict, engaged in a struggle to become herself.

To do so, Isak Dinesen had to define what her own life meant: not in relation to a husband, a lover, a coffee farm, or a noble name, but as the sum of her unique qualities and desires. In that process, Africa played a godparent's role. It gave her the privilege of a second childhood—not in the conventional sense, as a period of frivolous escapades, but as a time of awe. It gave her the opportunity for courage, and to trust her instincts. It gave her a sense of obligation and solidarity that in Denmark she had both longed for and scorned. And it gave her the knowledge that each one of us is, when the lion growls in the high grass, alone with her own wits, her own fleas, her own strength and weakness, her own mortality.

That lesson is a great privilege. When you have grasped it, you are fairly safe as to what can happen to you in life. You may lose the *things* that you hold dear: your lover, your health, your coffee farm, even your life. But you will be secure in your possession of the thing with the greatest and perhaps the only value: experience itself.

In 1960, *Life* magazine offered to send Isak Dinesen back to Kenya. The assignment was to cover the struggle for independence, which she had been following with the most fervent "prayers" for the Africans. She was, for a while, enormously tempted and excited

"I said good-bye to each of my house-boys, and, as I went out, they . . . left the door wide open behind me . . . as if they meant that I was to come back again . . ." (from Out of Africa).
BY PETER BEARD.

by the idea of going back, but after much hesitation she declined.

It was probably a wise decision. This was the woman who had refused the chance to live on in her farmhouse after her land was divided, telling the young developer who had made the offer that she would prefer to live in the middle of the Sahara Desert. How would she have felt to drive out of Nairobi, along the road to "Karen," which was now lined with suburban villas, and to find her coffee *shambas* turned into a golf course? How would she have regarded the glow of neon globes advertising imported car parts on the skyline of Nairobi? Or the omnipresence, in her hotel, of businessmen selling progress and tourists enthusing about their morning game drives?

While making up her mind about the dangers of a return, Dinesen had written to her nephew, Gustaf Blixen-Finecke, who was still farming outside Nairobi. "Kenya and my relations with the Natives have meant so much to me that I think it would round out my whole existence beautifully and harmoniously, if I could, again, if only for a short time, stand face to face with it altogether. But . . . I feel it would be just so pretentious and meaningless to sit crestfallen in Nairobi, with no real connection to the earth around it. . . ."

No real connection to the earth around it. When you first get out of an African town into the bush, you are struck by how deep and vast, yet how vital, the stillness is. It is as when a loudly droning, invisible machine is shut off—one that you were not conscious of hearing. You realize that the landscape is breathing, and that the stones giving off their heat, the ground giving up its moisture, the rhythms of individual breaths—animal and plant—are a kind of music. As your ears adjust, the sense of your own "real connection to the earth" catches you by surprise. It is a feeling of almost indescribable well-being, of having a secret wish granted; it is a feeling of connection to a body.

At that moment, the idea of breaking up the earth into parcels of real estate that can be traded, stolen, and fought over; into battlefields and minefields; into parking lots, slums, waste dumps, enemy territories, is an absurdity.

Perhaps it is a grand and impractical idea to believe that we can safeguard the "earth": the wilderness, the game, the freedom of tribal people to live as they always have. We can, though, safeguard what they mean to us—by imagining what it would mean to lose them. I think it would have pleased Isak Dinesen to know that, in her hundredth year, her "life and words" had helped keep alive the connection.

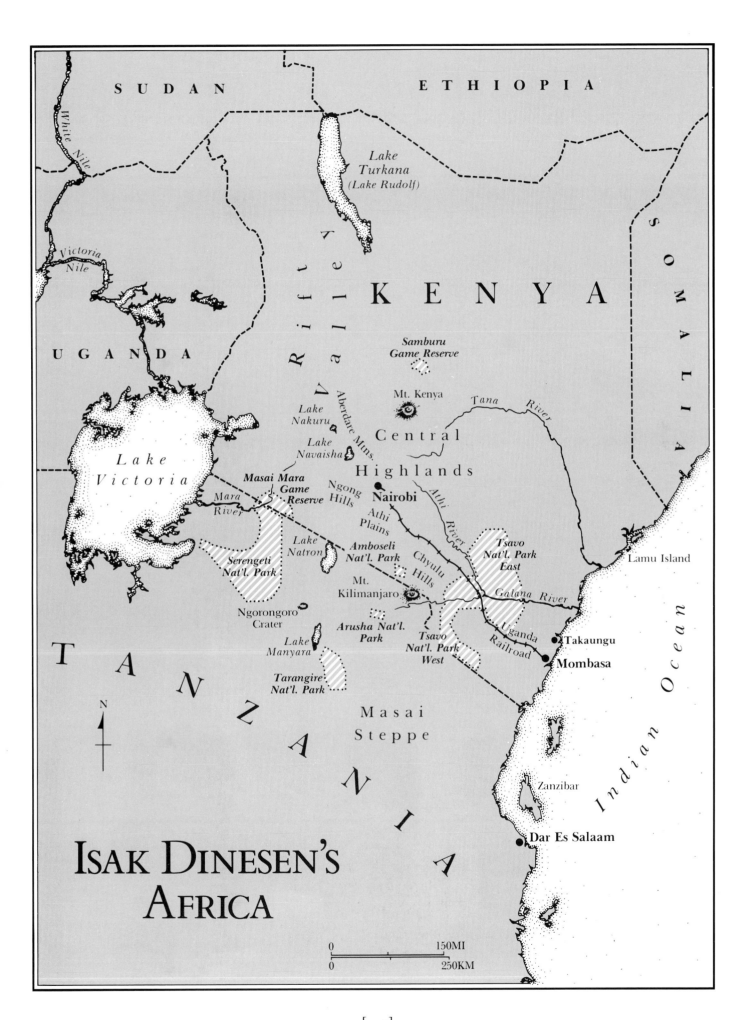

SUDAN

ETHIOPIA

White Nile

Victoria Nile

Lake Turkana (Lake Rudolf)

KENYA

SOMALIA

UGANDA

Victoria Nile

Samburu Game Reserve

Mt. Kenya

Tana River

Lake Nakuru

Aberdare Mtns.

Central

Lake Naivasha

Highlands

Lake Victoria

Masai Mara Game Reserve

Ngong Hills

Nairobi

Athi River

Mara River

Lake Natron

Athi Plains

Amboseli Nat'l. Park

Chyulu Hills

Tsavo Nat'l. Park East

Lamu Island

Serengeti Nat'l. Park

Mt. Kilimanjaro

Galana River

Ngorongoro Crater

Arusha Nat'l. Park

Tsavo Nat'l. Park West

Uganda Railroad

Takaungu

Mombasa

Lake Manyara

Masai Steppe

Tarangire Nat'l. Park

T A N Z A N I A

N

Zanzibar

Indian Ocean

Dar Es Salaam

Isak Dinesen's Africa

0   150MI

0   250KM

PART ONE

Into
the
Country

[EDITOR'S NOTE]

In December 1913, Karen Dinesen (known to her family and friends as Tanne) sailed from Denmark on the SS Admiral to the British East African port of Mombasa to join her fiancé, the Swedish Baron Bror Blixen-Finecke. The engaged couple emigrated to the colony, in what is now Kenya, to escape the provincial restraints of their Scandinavian backgrounds and at the urging of relatives who foresaw great opportunities there. Bror had preceded Tanne to Africa to acquire land, cattle, and a home; soon he wrote that he had abandoned the idea of cattle-raising in favor of coffee-farming. The baron would eventually prove to be an indifferent farmer and an incompatible husband for Tanne, but at this early stage they were affectionate partners, bonded by a commitment to their adventurous new life.

Bror and Tanne were married the day after her arrival in Mombasa, and that same afternoon they boarded the Uganda Railroad for the 300-mile journey from the seacoast to their new farm in the central highlands, near Nairobi. The train journey provided the new Baroness Blixen's first sight of East Africa's spectacular landscapes, at that time still densely populated with wild animals in vast herds. As her biographer, Judith Thurman, writes, "Nowhere on earth did life offer such a spectacle of vigor, beauty, harmony, and, above all, scale. It evoked a feeling of religious awe, a sense of gratitude in many of those who beheld it for the first time. . . . Looking back on her life in Africa, Karen Blixen felt 'that it might altogether be described as the existence of a person who had come from a rushed and noisy world, into a still country.' "

I HAD A FARM in Africa, at the foot of the Ngong Hills. The Equator runs across these highlands, a hundred miles to the North, and the farm lay at an altitude of over six thousand feet. In the day-time you felt that you had got high up, near to the sun, but the early mornings and evenings were limpid and restful, and the nights were cold.

The geographical position, and the height of the land combined to create a landscape that had not its like in all the world. There was no fat on it and no luxuriance anywhere; it was Africa distilled up through six thousand feet, like the strong and refined essence of a continent.

. . . The colours were dry and burnt, like the colours in pottery. The trees had a light delicate foliage, the structure of which was different from that of the trees in Europe; it did not grow in bows or cupolas, but in horizontal layers, and the formation gave to the tall solitary trees a likeness to the palms, or a heroic and romantic air like full-rigged ships with their sails clewed up, and to the edge of a wood a strange appearance as if the whole wood were faintly vibrating. Upon the grass of the great plains the crooked bare old thorn-trees were scattered, and the grass was spiced like thyme and bog-myrtle; in some places the scent was so strong, that it smarted in the nostrils.

THE CHIEF FEATURE of the landscape, and of your life in it, was the air. Looking back on a sojourn in the African highlands, you are struck by your feeling of having lived for a time up in the air. The sky was rarely more than pale blue or violet, with a profusion of mighty, weightless, ever-changing clouds towering up and sailing on it, but it has a blue vigour in it, and at a short distance it painted the ranges of hills and the woods a fresh deep blue. In the middle of the day the air was alive over the land, like a flame burning; it scintillated, waved and shone like running water, mirrored and doubled all objects, and created great Fata Morgana. Up in this high air you breathed easily, drawing in a vital assurance and lightness of heart. In the highlands you woke up in the morning and thought: Here I am, where I ought to be.

[TO INGEBORG DINESEN]

. . . Now we have caught sight of Africa on the horizon, and I hope that the dearly beloved country will greet me with the same friendliness that I feel for it. —I do feel that it is there that my life lies; the nearer I get to it, the closer seem the bonds that bind me to it. . . .

WHEN YOU FIRST COME to the country, landing at Mombasa, you will see, amongst the old light-grey Baobab-trees, — which look not like any earthly kind of vegetation but like porous fossilizations, gigantic belemnites, — grey stone ruins of houses, minarets and wells. The same sort of ruins are to be found all the way up the coast, at Takaunga, Kalifi and Lamu. They are the remnants of the towns of the ancient Arab traders in ivory and slaves.

The dhows of the traders knew all the African fairways, and trod the blue paths to the central market-place of Zanzibar. They were familiar with it at the time when Aladdin sent to the Sultan four hundred black slaves loaded with jewels, and when the Sultana feasted with her Negro lover while her husband was hunting, and was put to death for it.

. . . Probably, as these great merchants grew rich, they brought their harems with them to Mombasa and Kalifi, and themselves remained in their villas, by the long white breakers of the Ocean, and the flowering flaming trees, while they sent their expeditions up into the highlands.

[10]

. . . For from the wild hard country there, the scorched dry plains, and unknown waterless stretches, from the land of the broad thorn-trees along the rivers, and the diminutive, strong-smelling wild flowers of the black soil, came their wealth. Here, upon the roof of Africa, wandered the heavy, wise, majestic bearer of the ivory. He was deep in his own thoughts and wanted to be left to himself. But he was followed, and shot with poisoned arrows by the little dark Wanderobos, and with long, muzzle-loaded, silver-inlaid guns by the Arabs; he was trapped and thrown into pits all for the sake of his long smooth lightbrown tusks, that they sat and waited for it at Zanzibar.

MOMBASA HAS ALL the look of a picture of Paradise, painted by a small child. The deep Sea-arm round the island forms an ideal harbour; the land is made out of whitish coral-cliff grown with broad green mango trees and fantastic bald grey Baobab trees. The Sea at Mombasa is as blue as a cornflower, and, outside the inlet to the harbour, the long breakers of the Indian Ocean draw a thin crooked white line, and give out a low thunder even in the calmest weather. The narrow-streeted town of Mombasa is all built from coral-rock, in pretty shades of buff, rose and ochre, and above the town rises the massive old Fortress, with walls and embrasure, where three hundred years ago the Portuguese and the Arabs held out against one another; it displays stronger colours than the town, as if it had, in the course of the ages, from its high site drunk in more than one stormy sunset.

The flamboyant red Acacia flowers in the gardens of Mombasa, unbelievably intense of colour and delicate of leaf. The sun burns and scorches Mombasa; the air is salt here, the breeze brings in every day fresh supplies of brine from the East, and the soil itself is salted so that very little grass grows, and the ground is bare like a dancing-floor. But the ancient mango trees have a dense dark-green foliage and give benignant shade; they create a circular pool of black coolness underneath them.

. . . More than any other tree that I know of, they suggest a place to meet in, a centre for human intercourse; they are as sociable as the village-wells. Big markets are held under the mango trees, and the ground round their trunks is covered with hen-coops, and piled up water-melons.

I'LL BEGIN AT THE BEGINNING.—Bror was in Mombasa to meet me and it was wonderful to be with someone one feels one belongs with again, but Mombasa is a fiery hothouse and the sun blazing down on your head almost makes you unconscious. We went up to look at a very attractive old fort, and at eleven o'clock we were married, with Sjøgren, Prince Vilhelm, Bostrøm and Lewenhaupt standing as witnesses; it was extremely easy and simple and only took ten minutes at most. Then we drove out by ricksha to have lunch with Hobley, who had married us; he had a really delightful villa right on the shore,—and from there to the train, a special train for Prince Vilhelm, with the Governor's private dining car and Macmillan's chef and kitchen, which was absolutely splendid. To begin with it was fearfully hot, but toward evening it grew cooler. There is no sleeping car, but Bror had brought sheets and blankets.

. . . By the following morning the landscape had completely changed and then it was the real Africa, vast grass plains and the mountains in the distance and then an incredible wealth of game, huge flocks of zebra and gnu and antelope right beside the train, and although when you hear about that you don't attach much importance to it, when you see it for yourself you find it really impressive.—

IN NAIROBI there was an official reception and luncheon with the
Governor at his charming house, —I had the Governor on my
right and the Vice-Governor on my left and everyone called me
Baroness every other word; to start with I didn't realize they were
addressing me. I must admit that it was a pretty exhausting experience after a 24-hour train journey, with crowds of people I had never
seen before. —Immediately after lunch Bror and I drove out by car to
our own farm. It is the most enchanting road you can imagine, like
our own Deer Park, and the long blue range of the Ngong Hills
stretching out beyond it. There are so many flowering trees and
shrubs, and a scent rather like bog myrtle, or pine trees, pervades
everything. Out here it is not too hot at all, the air is so soft and
lovely, and one feels so light and free and happy.

There was a surprise in store for me when we arrived at the
farm. All the thousand boys were drawn up in ranks and after a really
ear-splitting welcome they closed ranks and came up to the house
with us, surrounded us when we got out of the car and insisted on
touching us, —and all those black heads right in front of one's gaze
were quite overwhelming. You have no idea how delightful the farm
was and how beautifully everything had been done up. I think the
garden can be made delightful; for there are fine trees and it is so
beautifully situated. . . .

[19]

NAIROBI WAS OUR TOWN, twelve miles away, down on a flat bit of land amongst hills. Here were the Government House and the big central offices; from here the country was ruled.

It is impossible that a town will not play a part in your life, it does not even make much difference whether you have more good or bad things to say of it, it draws your mind to it, by a mental law of gravitation. The luminous haze on the sky above the town at night, which I could see from some places on my farm, set my thoughts going, and recalled the big cities of Europe.

When I first came to Africa, there were no cars in the country, and we rode in to Nairobi, or drove in a cart with six mules to it, and stabled our animals in the stables of *The Highland Transport*. During all my time, Nairobi was a motley place, with some fine new stone buildings, and whole quarters of old corrugated iron shops, offices and bungalows, laid out with long rows of Eucalyptus trees along the bare dusty streets.

. . . All the same Nairobi was a town; here you could buy things, hear news, lunch or dine at the hotels and dance at the Club. And it was a live place, in movement like running water, and in growth like a young thing, it changed from year to year, and while you were away on a shooting Safari.

. . . The new Government House was built, a stately cool house with
a fine ball-room and a pretty garden, big hotels grew up, great impressive agricultural shows and fine flower shows were held, our
Quasi Smart Set of the Colony from time to time enlivened the town
with rows of quick melodrama. Nairobi said to you: "Make the most
of me and of time. Wir kommen nie wieder so jung—so undisciplined
and rapacious—zusammen." Generally I and Nairobi were in very
good understanding, and at one time I drove through the town and
thought: There is no world without Nairobi's streets.

PART TWO

The Farm in the Ngong Hills

[EDITOR'S NOTE]

Bror and Karen Blixen's first home in British East Africa was a modest farmhouse called Mbagathi, on 4,500 acres at the foot of the Ngong Hills. In 1917 they acquired an additional 1,500 acres and a larger house, a fieldstone manor that the Africans called Mbogani, or "forest house," which Tanne would occupy until her final departure from Africa in 1931. Her home and its surroundings are evocatively described in Out of Africa:

"My dining-room looked West, and had three long windows that opened out to the paved terrace, the lawn and the forest. The land here sloped down to the river that formed the boundary between me and the Masai. You could not see the river itself from the house, but you could follow its winding course by the design of the dark-green big Acacias which grew along it. To the other side of it the wood-clad land rose again, and over the woods were the green plains that reached to the foot of the Ngong Hills."

In that dining room, Karen Blixen entertained many of the region's European settlers, whose society centered on such visits to each others' farms, scattered throughout the highlands. Frequent trips to Nairobi, to conduct business and purchase supplies, also relieved the colonists' isola-

tion, as did madcap evenings at the Muthaiga Country Club, founded in 1914 by Berkeley Cole and the hub of social life for the colony's elite.

Their early years in Kenya were times of turmoil for the Blixens. World War I took Bror and other farmers from their estates to aid in fighting German troops under the elusive General von Lettow on the Tanganyika border. (For a time, the Blixens, as Scandinavians, were suspected by some British colonists of being German sympathizers.) And in 1915, Tanne made the first of several voyages back to Denmark to be treated for the syphilis she contracted from her husband early in their marriage. Chronically unfaithful and deeply restless, Bror spent little time at Mbogani, and in 1921 the couple separated permanently, at his wish and that of Tanne's family, though against her own.

Despite these and other troubles—dominated by the failing finances of her coffee-growing enterprise—Karen Blixen's attachment to Africa and to her farm grew stronger through the years she resided there. In 1926 she wrote to her brother, Thomas Dinesen, "Much, perhaps most, of my heart is in this country. . . ."

From the Ngong Hills you have a unique view, you see to the South the vast plains of the great game-country that stretches all the way to Kilimanjaro; to the East and North the park-like country of the foot-hills with the forest behind them, and the undulating land of the Kikuyu-Reserve, which extends to Mount Kenya a hundred miles away,—a mosaic of little square maize-fields, banana-groves and grass-land, with here and there the blue smoke from a native village, a small cluster of peaked mole-casts. But towards the West, deep down, lies the dry, moon-like landscape of the African low country. The brown desert is irregularly dotted with the little marks of the thornbushes, the winding river-beds are drawn up with crooked dark-green trails; those are the woods of the mighty, wide-branching Mimosa-trees, with thorns like spikes; the cactus grows here, and here is the home of the Giraffe and the Rhino.

The hill-country itself, when you get into it, is tremendously big, picturesque and mysterious; varied with long valleys, thickets, green slopes and rocky crags. High up, under one of the peaks, there is even a bamboo-grove. There are springs and wells in the hills; I have camped up here by them.

T HE WIND IN THE highlands blows steadily from the North-North-East. It is the same wind that, down at the coasts of Africa and Arabia, they name the Monsoon, the East Wind, which was King Solomon's favourite horse. Up here it is felt as just the resistance of the air, as the Earth throws herself forward into space. The wind runs straight against the Ngong Hills, and the slopes of the hills would be the ideal place for setting up a glider, that would be lifted upwards by the currents, over the mountain top. The clouds, which were travelling with the wind, struck the side of the hill and hung round it, or were caught on the summit and broke into rain. But those that took a higher course and sailed clear of the reef, dissolved to the West of it, over the burning desert of the Rift Valley. Many times I have from my house followed these mighty processions advancing, and have wondered to see their proud floating masses, as soon as they had got over the hills, vanish in the blue air and be gone.

T HE MOUNTAIN OF Ngong stretches in a
long ridge from North to South, and is
crowned with four noble peaks like immovable darker blue waves against the sky. It rises
eight thousand feet above the Sea, and to the
East two thousand feet above the surrounding
country; but to the West the drop is deeper
and more precipitous,—the hills fall vertically
down towards the Great Rift Valley.

You've no idea how delightful it is becoming out here as the
work in the park and on the house progresses. One thing that
gives me great joy is that there is the most lovely bird song all around
the house, exactly like nightingales,—and I wonder whether they are
in fact nightingales? We have most of the migratory birds from home
here, swallows, which are just gathering now in big flocks ready to
fly away, and which you perhaps may see on the telegraph wires
along Strandvejen, and storks that stroll about the meadows on the
farm here just as if they were in a Danish marsh. Bror thinks we
should call the place Bird Song. I can't get the English to pronounce
Frydenlund,—*Fuglsang* even less I am sure—but the <u>natives</u> call
this house Bogani; it means The Forest, and that is a good name
for it, too. . . .

U P ON THE VERY ridge of the hills and on the four peaks themselves it was easy to walk; the grass was short as on a lawn,
with the grey stone in places breaking through the sward. Along the
ridge, up and down the peaks, like a gentle switchback, there ran a
narrow game-path. One morning, at the time that I was camped in
the hills, I came up here and walked along the path, and I found on it
fresh tracks and dung of a herd of Eland. The big peaceful animals
must have been up on the ridge at sunrise, walking in a long row, and
you cannot imagine that they had come for any other reason than just
to look, deep down on both sides, at the land below.

. . . In my day, the Buffalo, the Eland and the Rhino lived in the
Ngong Hills,—the very old Natives remembered a time when there
were Elephants there,—and I was always sorry that the whole Ngong
Mountain was not enclosed in the Game Reserve. Only a small part
of it was Game Reserve, and the beacon on the Southern peak
marked the boundary of it. When the Colony prospers and Nairobi,
the capital, grows into a big city, the Ngong Hills might have made a
matchless game park for it. But during my last years in Africa many
young Nairobi shop-people ran out into the hills on Sundays, on
their motor-cycles, and shot at anything they saw, and I believe that
the big game will have wandered away from the hills, through the
thorn-thickets and the stony ground further South.

ENCLOSED I AM sending you an everlasting flower that I picked on the summit
of the Ngong Hills, when I was up there with
Ette and Nisse and Ingrid's two eldest girls
last Thursday. It is so strange, I always feel
that the Ngong Hills, and especially the desert landscape you can see toward the west,
actually belong to you; I felt you were with us
the whole time, and I wonder whether you
by any chance had the feeling of being in the
mountains that day. Strangely enough at this
dry season there were masses of flowers up
there; whole slopes were completely yellow
with these everlasting flowers, and then there
was a little white clematis climbing about
over everything, that I had not seen before.

. . . When one gets right up on to the ridge
a path made by animals follows the crest,
trampled hard down and easy to walk on;
it is pleasant to visualize the buffalo, eland,
and other animals strolling along it, attracted by the enormous view on both sides.
A flock of eland had left it just ahead of us.

. . . We also saw a lot of bushbuck, and at a
great height a large number of eagles, as
there always are. But we did not get a
glimpse of any giraffe. We sat there on the
summit for a while and felt we were on the
peak of the whole world.

WE GREW COFFEE on my farm. The land was in itself a little too high for coffee, and it was hard work to keep it going; we were never rich on the farm. But a coffee-plantation is a thing that gets hold of you and does not let you go, and there is always something to do on it: you are generally just a little behind with your work.

In the wildness and irregularity of the country, a piece of land laid out and planted according to rule, looked very well. Later on, when I flew in Africa, and became familiar with the appearance of my farm from the air, I was filled with admiration for my coffee-plantation, that lay quite bright green in the grey-green land, and I realized how keenly the human mind yearns for geometrical figures.

. . . There are times of great beauty on a coffee-farm. When the plantation flowered in the beginning of the rains, it was a radiant sight, like a cloud of chalk, in the mist and the drizzling rain, over six hundred acres of land. The coffee-blossom has a delicate slightly bitter scent, like the blackthorn blossom. When the field reddened with the ripe berries, all the women and the children, whom they call the Totos, were called out to pick the coffee off the trees, together with the men; then the waggons and carts brought it down to the factory near the river. . . . Once the whole factory burned down and had to be built up again. The big coffee-dryer turned and turned, rumbling the coffee in its iron belly with a sound like pebbles that are washed about on the sea-shore. Sometimes the coffee would be dry, and ready to take out of the dryer, in the middle of the night. That was a picturesque moment, with many hurricane lamps in the huge dark room of the factory, that was hung everywhere with cobwebs and coffee-husks, and with eager glowing dark faces, in the light of the lamps, round the dryer; the factory, you felt, hung in the great African night like a bright jewel in an Ethiope's ear.

[41]

THE FARM-ROAD in one place ran through a wide cup of grassy ground, there was a spring here and I thought out the plan of building a dam below it and turning the place into a lake. You are always short of water in Africa, it would be a great gain to the cattle to be able to drink in the field, and save themselves the long journey down to the river. This idea of a dam occupied all the farm day and night, and was much discussed; in the end, when it was finished, it was to all of us a majestic achievement.

. . . In the course of time, I got a vast expanse of water here, seven feet deep in places; the road went through the pond, it was very pretty. Later on we even built two more dams lower down and in this way obtained a row of ponds, like pearls upon a string.

The pond now became the heart of the farm. It was always much alive, with a ring of cattle and children round it, and in the hot season, when water-holes dried up in the plains and the hills, the birds came to the farm: herons, ibis, kingfishers, quail, and a dozen varieties of geese and duck. In the evening, when the first stars sprang out in the sky, I used to go and sit by the pond, and then the birds came home.

AN AFRICAN NATIVE Forest is a mysterious region. You ride into the depths of an old tapestry, in places faded and in others darkened with age, but marvellously rich in green shades. You cannot see the sky at all in there, but the sunlight plays in many strange ways, falling through the foliage. The grey fungus, like long drooping beards, on the trees, and the creepers hanging down everywhere, give a secretive, recondite air to the Native forest. I used to ride here with Farah on Sundays, when there was nothing to do on the farm, up and down the slopes, and across the little winding forest-streams. The air in the forest was cool like water, and filled with the scent of plants, and in the beginning of the long rains when the creepers flowered, you rode through sphere after sphere of fragrance.

. . . One kind of African Daphne of the woods, which flowers with a small cream-coloured sticky blossom, had an overwhelming sweet perfume, like lilac, and wild lily of the valley. Here and there, hollow tree-stems were hung up in ropes of hide on a branch; the Kikuyu hung them there to make the bees build in them, and to get honey. Once as we turned a corner in the forest, we saw a leopard sitting on the road, a tapestry animal.

Here, high above the ground, lived a garrulous restless nation, the little grey monkeys. Where a pack of monkeys had travelled over the road, the smell of them lingered for a long time in the air, a dry and stale, mousy smell. As you rode on you would suddenly hear the rush and whizz over your head, as the colony passed along on its own ways. If you kept still in the same place for some time you might catch sight of one of the monkeys sitting immovable in a tree, and, a little after, discover that the whole forest round you was alive with his family, placed like fruits on the branches, grey or dark figures according to how the sunlight fell on them, all with their long tails hanging down behind them.

. . . In the Ngong Forest I have also seen, on a narrow path through
thick growth, in the middle of a very hot day, the Giant Forest
Hog, a rare person to meet. He came suddenly past me, with his
wife and three young pigs, at a great speed, the whole family
looking like uniform, bigger and smaller figures cut out in dark
paper, against the sunlit green behind them. It was a glorious sight,
like a reflection in a forest pool, like a thing that had happened a
thousand years ago.

LULU CAME TO MY house from the woods . . . a young antelope of the bushbuck tribe, which is perhaps the prettiest of all the African antelopes. They are a little bigger than the fallow-deer; they live in the woods, or in the bush, and are shy and fugitive, so that they are not seen as often as the antelopes of the plains. But the Ngong Hills, and the surrounding country, were good places for bushbuck, and if you had your camp in the hills . . . you would see them come out of the bush into the glades, and as the rays of the sun fell upon them their coats shone red as copper. The male has a pair of delicately turned horns.

[*When the author found her,*] Lulu was only as big as a cat, with large quiet purple eyes. She had such delicate legs that you feared they would not bear being folded up and unfolded again, as she lay down and rose up. Her ears were smooth as silk and exceedingly expressive. Her nose was as black as a truffle. Her diminutive hoofs gave her all the air of a young Chinese lady of the old school, with laced feet. It was a rare experience to hold such a perfect thing in your hands. . . . On the strength of this great beauty and gracefulness, Lulu obtained for herself a commanding position in the house, and was treated with respect by all.

The league between Lulu and her family and my house lasted for many years. The bushbucks were often in the neighbourhood of the house, they came out of the woods and went back again as if my grounds were a province of the wild country. They came mostly just before sunset, and first moved in amongst the trees like delicate dark silhouettes on the dark green, but when they stepped out to graze on the lawn in the light of the afternoon sun their coats shone like copper.

. . . It also seemed to me that the free union between my house and the antelope was a rare, honourable thing. Lulu came in from the wild world to show that we were on good terms with it, and she made my house one with the African landscape, so that nobody could tell where the one stopped and the other began. Lulu knew the place of the Giant Forest-Hog's lair and had seen the Rhino copulate. In Africa there is a cuckoo which sings in the middle of the hot days in the midst of the forest, like the sonorous heartbeat of the world, I had never had the luck to see her, neither had anyone that I knew, for nobody could tell me how she looked. But Lulu had perhaps walked on a narrow green deerpath just under the branch on which the cuckoo was sitting.

I N NORMAL YEARS the long rains began in the last week of March
and went on into the middle of June. Up to the time of the rains,
the world grew hotter and drier every day, feverish, as in Europe
before a great thunderstorm, only more so.
. . . Gigantic clouds gathered, and dissolved again, over the landscape; a light distant shower of rain painted a blue slanting streak
across the horizon. All the world had only one thought.

On an evening just before sunset, the scenery drew close round
you, the hills came near and were vigorous, meaningful, in their
clear, deep blue and green colouring. A couple of hours later you
went out and saw that the stars had gone, and you felt the night-air
soft and deep and pregnant with benefaction.

When the quickly growing rushing sound wandered over your head it was the wind in the tall forest-trees,—and not the rain. When it ran along the ground it was the wind in the shrubs and the long grass,—and not the rain. When it rustled and rattled just above the ground it was the wind in the maize-fields,—where it sounded so much like rain that you were taken in, time after time, and even got a certain content from it, as if you were at least shown the thing you longed for acted on a stage,—and not the rain.

But when the earth answered like a sounding-board in a deep fertile roar, and the world sang round you in all dimensions, all above and below,—that was the rain. It was like coming back to the Sea, when you have been a long time away from it, like a lover's embrace.

B UT ONE YEAR the long rains failed. It was, then, as if the Universe were turning away from you. It grew cooler, on some days it would be cold, but there was no sign of moisture in the atmosphere. Everything became drier and harder, and it was as if all force and gracefulness had withdrawn from the world. It was not bad weather or good weather, but a negation of all weather, as if it had been deferred *sine die*. A bleak wind, like a draught, ran over your head, all colour faded from all things; the smells went away from the fields and forests. The feeling of being in disgrace with the Great Powers pressed on you. To the South, the burnt plains lay black and waste, striped with grey and white ashes.

On the plains and in the hills, the waterholes dried up, and many new kinds of ducks and geese came to my pond. To the pond on the boundary of the farm, the Zebra came wandering in the early mornings and at sunset to drink, in long rows, two or three hundred of them, the foals walking with the mares, and they were not afraid of me when I rode out amongst them. But we tried to keep them off the land for the sake of our cattle, for the water was sinking in the ponds. Still it was a pleasure to go down there, where the rushes growing in the mud made a green patch in the brown landscape.

[53]

WE HAVE HAD RAIN!! More than 4″ in three days, and no one could imagine what a difference it makes to the shamba,— and so to the whole of life! . . . Perhaps now our time of tribulation is really over and better times are on the way. Now even the furthest, deepest valley is turning green, —it is something of a miracle how quickly everything here is transformed by the rain; the Ngong Hills and the Reserve, that were burned to the likeness of a doormat, are now brilliant with the finest, most glorious green, and the whole shamba is flowering. If only it will go on. . . . It is so beautiful here, a para- dise on earth, when there is enough rain. And in a way, during the times of tribulation one comes to love this intractable country still more; I have a feeling that wherever I may be in the future, I will be wondering whether there is rain at Ngong.

WE HAD MANY visitors to the farm. In Pioneer countries hospitality is a necessity of life not to the travellers alone but to the settlers. A visitor is a friend, he brings news, good or bad, which is bread to the hungry minds in lonely places. A real friend who comes to the house is a heavenly messenger, who brings the *panis angelorum*.

When Denys Finch-Hatton came back after one of his long expeditions, he was starved for talk, and found me on the farm starved for talk, so that we sat over the dinner-table into the small hours of the morning, talking of all the things we could think of, and mastering them all, and laughing at them. White people, who for a long time live alone with Natives, get into the habit of saying what they mean, because they have no reason or opportunity for dissimulation, and when they meet again their conversation keeps the Native tone. We then kept up the theory that the wild Masai tribe, in their manyatta under the hills, would see the house all afire, like a star in the night, as the peasants of Umbria saw the house wherein Saint Francis and Saint Clare were entertaining one another upon theology.

To the great wanderers amongst my friends, the farm owed its charm, I believe, to the fact that it was stationary and remained the same whenever they came to it. They had been over vast countries and had raised and broken their tents in many places, now they were pleased to round my drive that was steadfast as the orbit of a star. They liked to be met by familiar faces, and I had the same servants all the time that I was in Africa. I had been on the farm longing to get away, and they came back to it longing for books and linen sheets and the cool atmosphere in a big shuttered room; by their campfires they had been meditating upon the joys of farm life, and as they arrived they asked me eagerly: "Have you taught your cook to make an *omelette à la chasseur?*—and have the gramophone records from 'Petrouchka' arrived by the last mail?" They came and stayed in the house also when I was away, and Denys had the use of it, when I was on a visit in Europe. "My Silvan Retreat," Berkeley Cole called it.

As far as Berkeley Cole and Denys Finch-Hatton were concerned, my house was a communist establishment. Everything in it was theirs, and they took a pride in it, and brought home the things they felt to be lacking. They kept the house up to a high standard in wine and tobacco, and got books and gramophone records out from Europe for me.

. . . Berkeley, like his brother Galbraith Cole and his brother-in-law Lord Delamere, was an early settler, a pioneer of the Colony, and intimate with the Masai, who in those days were the domineering nation of the land. He had known them before the European civilization,—which in the depths of their hearts they loathed more than anything else in the world,—cut through their roots; before they were moved from their fair North country. He could speak with them of the old days in their own tongue. Whenever Berkeley was staying on the farm, the Masai came over the river to see him. The old chiefs sat and discussed their troubles of the present time with him, his jokes would make them laugh, and it was as if a hard stone had laughed.

Berkeley, if he had had his small head enriched with a wig of long silky curls, could have walked in and out of the Court of King Charles II. . . . I felt that the law of gravitation did not apply to Berkeley, but that he might, as we sat talking at night by the fire, at any moment go straight up through the chimney.

BERKELEY COLE

 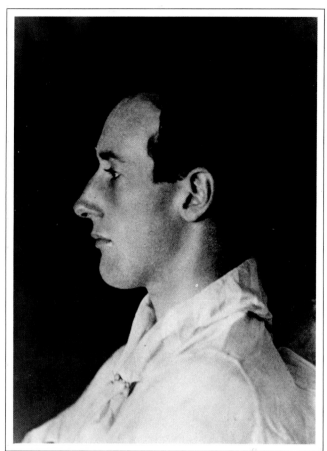

DENYS FINCH HATTON

. . . If Berkeley were a cavalier of the Stuarts' day, Denys [Finch-Hatton] should be set in an earlier English landscape, in the days of Queen Elizabeth. He could have walked arm in arm, there, with Sir Philip, or Francis Drake. And the people of Elizabeth's time might have held him dear because to them he would have suggested that Antiquity, the Athens, of which they dreamed and wrote. Denys could indeed have been placed harmoniously in any period of our civilization, *tout comme chez soi*, all up till the opening of the nineteenth century. He would have cut a figure in any age, for he was an athlete, a musician, a lover of art and a fine sportsman. He did cut a figure in his own age, but it did not quite fit in anywhere. His friends in England always wanted him to come back, they wrote out plans and schemes for a career for him there, but Africa was keeping him.

. . . The particular, instinctive attachment which all Natives of Africa felt towards Berkeley and Denys, and towards a few other people of their kind, made me reflect that perhaps the white men of the past, indeed of any past, would have been in better understanding and sympathy with the coloured races than we, of our Industrial Age, shall ever be. When the first steam engine was constructed, the roads of the races of the world parted, and we have never found one another since.

SOMETIMES a cool, colourless day in the months after the rainy season calls back the time of the *marka mbaya*, the bad year, the time of the drought. In those days the Kikuyu used to graze their cows round my house, and a boy amongst them who had a flute, from time to time played a short tune on it. When I have heard this tune again, it has recalled in one single moment all our anguish and despair of the past. It has got the salt taste of tears in it. But at the same time I found in the tune, unexpectedly, surprisingly, a vigour, a curious sweetness, a song. Had those hard times really had all these in them? There was youth in us then, a wild hope. It was during those long days that we were all of us merged into a unity, so that on another planet we shall recognise one another, and the things cry to each other, the cuckoo clock and my books to the lean-fleshed cows on the lawn and the sorrowful old Kikuyus: "You also were there. You also were part of the Ngong farm." That bad time blessed us and went away.

The friends of the farm came to the house, and went away again. They were not the kind of people who stay for a long time in the same place. They were not the kind of people either who grow old, they died and never came back. But they had sat contented by the fire, and when the house, closing round them, said: "I will not let you go except you bless me," they laughed and blessed it, and it let them go.

PART THREE

Africa in Flesh and Blood

[EDITOR'S NOTE]

Karen Blixen's fascination with the people of Africa was immediate and enduring, "a magnificent enlargement of all my world," as she wrote in Out of Africa. Her relationship with the Africans was compounded from several strains: her strong attraction to the exotic, her perception of the people as a direct link with the country's wildness, and her dependence on them for aid and companionship, especially after her marriage ended.

Some three million natives, belonging to many tribes, lived in Kenya when she arrived. Most of those living on her farm, in villages called shambas, were Kikuyus, who had farmed the central highlands for generations before the white settlers came. Close by, on the reserve to which they had been displaced from more northerly homelands, were the proud and fierce Masai, a herding and hunting nation both admired and feared by the Europeans for their belligerence. Another nomadic and often violent people were the devoutly Muslim Somalis, emigrants from coastal regions to the northeast; unlike the Masai, though, the sophisticated Somalis frequently became trusted servants of Africa's new rulers.

Certain members of Karen Blixen's household staff were most important to her existence in Africa. The Somali Farah Aden, originally Bror's steward, was Tanne's escort on the final stage of her maiden voyage to Kenya; until her departure eighteen years later he served as her major domo, interpreter, facilitator, and confidant. They remained in contact, Farah reporting to Tanne on the lives of "her" people, until his death in the early 1940s. Juma bin Mohammed, half Somali, half Masai, remained for the length of Tanne's sojourn and raised his children on the farm. And "a small Kikuyu boy" named Kamante Gatura was taken into her household after she helped to cure his diseased leg, and stayed on as her gifted chef de cuisine. Perhaps the most picturesque and complex personality in Dinesen's African chronicles, Kamante still lives near the farm as of this writing, and will live for much longer in the minds of her readers.

Karen Blixen's passion for the Africans does not, as Judith Thurman notes, alter the fact "that her relations with them were feudal, that her knowledge of their customs and history was circumstantial, or that her vantage point was both romantic and paternalistic. Yet she saw, without any urging, the 'dignity and value' of their arts. She grasped . . . that wisdom which could create a moral order so much more functional than that of her own race." She also foresaw the devastating social and psychological impact that colonization would have on Africa: "We Nations of Europe . . . who do not fear to floodlight our own inmost mechanisms, are here turning the blazing lights of civilization into dark eyes. . . . If for a long enough time we continue in this way to dazzle and blind the Africans, we may in the end bring upon them a longing for darkness, which will drive them into the gorges of their own, unknown mountains and their own, unknown minds." (Shadows on the Grass)

WHEN YOU HAVE caught the rhythm of Africa, you find that it is the same in all her music. What I learned from the game of the country, was useful to me in my dealings with the Native People.

. . . The discovery of the dark races was to me a magnificent enlargement of all my world. If a person with an inborn sympathy for animals had grown up in a milieu where there were no animals, and had come into contact with animals late in life; or if a person with an instinctive taste for woods and forest had entered a forest for the first time at the age of twenty; or if some one with an ear for music had happened to hear music for the first time when he was already grown up; their cases might have been similar to mine. After I had met with the Natives, I set out the routine of my daily life to the Orchestra.

ON OUR SAFARIS, and on the farm, my acquaintance with the Natives developed into a settled and personal relationship. We were good friends. I reconciled myself to the fact that while I should never quite know or understand them, they knew me through and through, and were conscious of the decisions that I was going to take, before I was certain about them myself. For some time I had a small farm up at Gil-Gil, where I lived in a tent, and I travelled by the railway to and fro between Gil-Gil and Ngong. At Gil-Gil, I might make up my mind very suddenly, when it began to rain, to go back to my house. But when I came to Kikuyu, which was our station on the railway line, and from where it was ten miles to the farm, one of my people would be there with a mule for me to ride home on. When I asked them how they had known that I was coming down, they looked away, and seemed uneasy, as if frightened or bored, such as we should be if a deaf person insisted on getting an explanation of a symphony from us.

. . . The Natives have, far less than the white people, the sense of risks in life. Sometimes on a Safari, or on the farm, in a moment of extreme tension, I have met the eyes of my Native companions, and have felt that we were at a great distance from one another, and that they were wondering at my apprehension of our risk. It made me reflect that perhaps they were, in life itself, within their own element, such as we can never be, like fishes in deep water which for the life of them cannot understand our fear of drowning. This assurance, this art of swimming, they had, I thought, because they had preserved a knowledge that was lost to us by our first parents; Africa, amongst the continents, will teach it to you: that God and the Devil are one, the majesty coeternal, not two uncreated but one uncreated, and the Natives neither confounded the persons nor divided the substance.

I HAD SIX THOUSAND acres of land, and had thus got much spare land besides the coffee-plantation. Part of the farm was native forest, and about one thousand acres were squatters' land, what they called their *shambas*. The squatters are Natives, who with their families hold a few acres on a white man's farm, and in return have to work for him a certain number of days in the year. My squatters, I think, saw the relationship in a different light, for many of them were born on the farm, and their fathers before them, and they very likely regarded me as a sort of superior squatter on their estates.

The squatters' land was more intensely alive than the rest of the farm, and was changing with the seasons the year round. The maize grew up higher than your head as you walked on the narrow hard-trampled footpaths in between the tall green rustling regiments, and then again it was harvested. The beans ripened in the fields, were gathered and thrashed by the women, and the stalks and pods were collected and burned, so that in certain seasons thin blue columns of smoke rose here and there all over the farm. The Kikuyu also grew the sweet potatoes, that have a vine-like leaf and spread over the ground like a dense entangled mat, and many varieties of big yellow and green speckled pumpkins.

WHENEVER YOU WALK amidst the Kikuyu shambas, the first thing that will catch your eye is the hind part of a little old woman raking in her soil, like a picture of an ostrich which buries her head in the sand. Each Kikuyu family had a number of small round peaked huts and store-huts; the space between the huts was a lively place, the earth hard as concrete; here the maize was ground and the goats milked, and children and chickens were running. I used to shoot spurfowl in the sweet-potato fields round the squatters' houses in the blue late afternoons, and the stock-pigeons cooed out a loud song in the high-stemmed, fringy trees, which were left over, here and there in the shambas, from the forest that had once covered all the farm.

The old women of the farm were all good friends of mine. I saw less of them than of the small restless totos, who were ever about my house, but they had agreed to assume the existence of a particular understanding and intimacy between them and me, as if they had all been aunties of mine. Kikuyu women with age shrink and grow darker; seen beside the cinnamon-coloured Nditos, sap-filled, sleek lianas of the forest, they look like sticks of charcoal, weightless, desiccated all through, with a kind of grim jocosity at the core of them, noble, high-class achievements of the skilled charcoal-burner of existence.

T HE GREATEST SOCIAL functions of the farm were the *Ngomas*,— the big Native dances. At these occasions we entertained up to fifteen hundred or two thousand guests.

. . . [T]he real performers, the indefatigable young dancers, brought the glory and luxury of the festivity with them, they were immune to foreign influence, and concentrated upon the sweetness and fire within themselves. One thing only did they demand from the outside world: a space of level ground to dance on. This was to be found near my house, the big lawn was plain under the trees, and the square, in the forest between my boys' huts, had been laid out level. For this reason the farm was highly thought of by the young people of the country, and the invitations to my balls much valued.

. . . The Kikuyu, when going to a Ngoma, rub themselves all over with a particular kind of pale red chalk, which is much in demand and is bought and sold; it gives them a strangely *blond* look. The colour is neither of the animal nor the vegetable world, in it the young people themselves look fossilized, like statues cut in rock. The girls in their demure, bead-embroidered, tanned leather garments cover these, as well as themselves, with the earth, and look all one with them,—clothed statues in which the folds and draperies are daintily carried out by a skilled artist. The young men are naked for an Ngoma, but on such occasions make much out of their coiffures, clapping the chalk on to their manes and pigtails, and carrying their limestone heads high. During my last years in Africa, the Government forbade the people to put chalk on the head. In both sexes the rig-out is of the greatest effect: diamonds and high decorations will not impart to their bearers a more decided gala appearance. Whenever at a distance you catch sight, in the landscape, of a group of red-chalked Kikuyu on the march, you feel the atmosphere vibrating with festivity.

THE NATIVES WERE Africa in flesh and
blood. The tall extinct volcano of
Longonot that rises above the Rift Valley, the
broad Mimosa trees along the rivers, the Elephant and the Giraffe, were not more truly
Africa than the Natives were,—small figures
in an immense scenery. All were different ex-
pressions of one idea, variations upon the
same theme. It was not a congenial upheaping
of heterogeneous atoms, but a heterogeneous
upheaping of congenial atoms, as in the case
of the oak-leaf and the acorn and the object
made from oak. We ourselves, in boots, and
in our constant great hurry, often jar with the
landscape. The Natives are in accordance
with it, and when the tall, slim, dark, and
dark-eyed people travel,—always one by one,
so that even the great Native veins of traffic
are narrow foot-paths,—or work the soil, or
herd their cattle, or hold their big dances, or
tell you a tale, it is Africa wandering, dancing
and entertaining you.

I HAD IN AFRICA many servants, whom I shall always remember as part of my existence there. There was Ismael, my gun-bearer, a mighty huntsman brought up and trained exclusively in the hunter's world, a great tracker and weather prophet, expressing himself in hunter's terminology and speaking of my "big" and my "young" rifle. It was Ismael who after his return to Somaliland addressed his letter to me "Lioness Blixen" and began it: "Honourable Lioness." There was old Ismael, my cook and faithful companion on safaris, who was a kind of Mohammedan saint. And there was Kamante, a small figure to look at but great, even formidable, in his total isolation. But Farah was my servant by the grace of God.

. . . Farah, although gravely posing as a highly respectable major-domo, Malvolio himself, was a wild animal, and nothing in the world would ever stand between him and God. Unfailingly loyal, he was still at heart a wild animal, a cheetah noiselessly following me about at a distance of five feet, or a falcon holding on to my finger with strong talons and turning his head right and left. The qualities with which he served me were cheetah or falcon qualities.

When Farah first took service in my house, or first took my house into possession—for from that day he spoke of "our house," "our horses," "our guests"—it was no common contract which was set up, but a covenant established between him and me *ad majorem domus gloriam*, to the ever greater glory of the house. My well-being was not his concern, and was hardly of real importance to him, but for my good name and prestige he did, I believe, hold himself responsible before God.

KAMANTE WAS A SMALL Kikuyu boy, the son of one of my squatters. . . . [W]hen I first met him [he] looked as if he were six years old, but he had a brother who looked about eight, and both brothers agreed that Kamante was the elder of them, so I suppose he must have been set back in growth by his long illness; he was probably then nine years old. He grew up now, but he always made the impression of being a dwarf, or in some way deformed, although you could not put your finger on the precise spot that made him look so. His angular face was rounded with time, he walked and moved easily, and I myself did not think him bad-looking, but I may have looked upon him with something of a creator's eyes. His legs remained forever as thin as sticks. A fantastic figure he always was, half of fun and half of diabolism; with a very slight alteration, he might have sat and stared down, on the top of the Cathedral of Notre Dame in Paris.

He had in him something bright and live; in a painting he would have made a spot of unusually intense colouring; with this he gave a stroke of picturesqueness to my household. He was never quite right in the head, or at least he was always what, in a white person, you would have called highly eccentric.

. . . Kamante began his life in my house as a dog-toto, later he became a medical assistant to me. There I found out what good hands he had, although you would not have thought so from the look of them, and I sent him into the kitchen to be a cook's boy, a marmiton, under my old cook Esa, who was murdered. After Esa's death he succeeded to him, and he was now my Chef all the time that he was with me. . . . I sent Kamante in to the Muthaiga Club to learn, and to the cooks of my friends in Nairobi, when I had had a new good dish in their house, and by the time that he had served his apprenticeship, my own house became famous in the Colony for its table.

T HE MASAI WERE my neighbours; if I rode across the river which formed the border of my farm I was in their Reserve. But the Masai themselves were not always there. They trekked with their big herds of cattle from one part of the grass-land—which was about the size of Ireland—to another, according to the rains and the condition of the grazing. When again they came round my way and set to patch up their huts of cow-hide for a sojourn of some time, they would send over to notify me, and I would ride over to call on them.

. . . Here lay before you a hundred miles' gallop over grass and open undulating land; there was not a fence nor a ditch, and no road. There was no human habitation except the Masai villages, and those were deserted half the year, when the great wanderers took themselves and their herds off to other pastures. There were low thorn trees regularly spread over the plain, and long deep valleys with dry riverbeds of big flat stones, where you had to find a deer-path here and there to take you across. After a little while you became aware of how still it was out here. Now, looking back on my life in Africa, I feel that it might altogether be described as the existence of a person who had come from a rushed and noisy world, into a still country.

A MASAI WARRIOR is a fine sight. Those young men have, to the utmost extent, that particular form of intelligence which we call *chic*;—daring, and wildly fantastical as they seem, they are still unswervingly true to their own nature, and to an immanent ideal. Their style is not an assumed manner, nor an imitation of a foreign perfection; it has grown from the inside, and is an expression of the race and its history, and their weapons and finery are as much part of their being as are a stag's antlers.

. . . The young Masai Morani live upon milk and blood; it is perhaps this diet that gives them their wonderful smoothness and silkiness of skin. Their faces, with the high cheek-bones and boldly swung jaw-bones, are sleek, without a line or groove in them, swollen; the dim unseeing eyes lie therein like two dark stones tightly fitted into a mosaic; altogether the young Morani have a likeness to mosaics. . . . The great contrast, or harmony, between these swollen smooth faces, full necks and broad rounded shoulders, and the surprising narrowness of their waist and hips, the leanness and spareness of the thigh and knee and the long, straight, sinewy leg give them the look of creatures trained through hard discipline to the height of rapaciousness, greed, and gluttony.

The Masai walk stiffly, placing one slim foot straight in front of the other, but their movements of arm, wrist and hand are very supple. When a young Masai shoots with a bow and arrow, and lets go the bow-string, you seem to hear the sinews of his long wrist singing in the air with the arrow.

T HE MASAI DID NOT like us and had no reason to do so. For we
had put an end to their bird-of-prey raids on the agricultural
tribes, we had taken their spears and their big almond-shaped shields
from them, and had splashed a bucket of water upon the halo of a
warrior nation, hardened through a thousand years into a personifica-
tion of that ideal of Nietzsche: "Man for war, and woman for the
warrior's delight, all else is foolishness."

Once when I was on safari deep in the Reserve, a very old Masai came up and seated himself by my campfire; after a while he began to speak, and it was like hearing a boulder speak. I myself spoke sufficient Masai to enquire about game and water, and no more. . . . But on my safaris I had an interpreter with me. "Nowadays," according to him, the Moran—warrior—of sixty years ago told us, "it is no pleasure to live. But in the old days it was good fun. When then the Kikuyu or the Wakamba had got a fat piece of land, and fat herds of cattle, goats and sheep on it, we Morani came to them. First we killed all men and male children with steel"—the Masai warriors had long, fine spears and short, strong swords—"and we were allowed to stay on in the village until we had eaten up the sheep and goats there. Then before going away again, we killed off the women with wood" —for the Masai also in their belts carried wooden clubs, surprisingly light and effective. I do not know if our old guest was actually calling up a past, or if in his long nocturnal monologue he was picturing to himself an ideal state of things, and was slowly getting drunk on his vision of it. He walked away at last and disappeared into the night, a bald, skinny bird of prey of a dying species.

[87]

ALL MY LIFE I have held that you can class people according to how they may be imagined behaving to King Lear. You could not reason with King Lear, any more than with an old Kikuyu, and from the first he demanded too much of everybody; but he was a king. It is true that the African Native has not handed over his country to the white man in a magnificent gesture, so that the case is in some ways different from that of the old king and his daughters; the white men took over the country as a Protectorate. But I bore in mind that not very long ago, at a time that could still be remembered, the Natives of the country had held their land undisputed, and had never heard of the white men and their laws. Within the general insecurity of their existence the land to them was still steadfast. . . . Those who were taken away, in their exile and thraldom all over the Eastern world, would long back to the highlands, for that was their own land. The old dark clear-eyed Native of Africa, and the old dark clear-eyed Elephant,—they are alike; you see them standing on the ground, weighty with such impressions of the world around them as have been slowly gathered. . . . Either one of the two might find himself quite perplexed by the sight of the great changes that are going on all round him, and might ask you where he was, and you would have to answer him in the words of Kent: "In your own kingdom, Sir."

[PART FOUR]

Safari

[EDITOR'S NOTE]

". . . [W]e often talked on the farm of the safaris that we had been on. Camping-places fix themselves in your mind as if you had spent long periods of your life in them. You will remember a curve of your wagon track in the grass of the plain, like the features of a friend." (Out of Africa)

For relief from the farm's shauries *(troubles), for physical refreshment, or just for the sense of liberation it offered, Karen Blixen often traveled out into the wild country of Kenya on safari. Bror Blixen was an insatiable sportsman, and after their divorce he supported himself chiefly by leading safaris. Several of Tanne's closest friends—such as the Swedish Baron Erik von Otter and the Englishman Denys Finch Hatton—also were among the noted hunters of their time, and she quickly caught their enthusiasm for safari life.*

Her books vividly describe the scenic abundance of Africa's wilderness: the great savannahs; "the park-like country of the foot-hills"; the deep mountain forests, winding rivers, and soda lakes; and "the dry, moon-like landscape of the African low country." The elemental qualities of safari life intoxicated Tanne, and in her appreciation of the rough pleasures of camping she seems more contemporary than most women of her day.

In her admiration for the wild animals, mingled with an undeniable blood lust, Karen Blixen was not unlike most settlers of that era. Her feeling about lions exemplified this seemingly conflicted attitude; it was the creature she could never resist trying to shoot, yet she could write this in a letter to her brother: "In their build, carriage and movements lions possess a greatness, a majesty, which . . . makes one feel later that everything else is so trivial—thousands of generations of unrestricted supreme authority, and one . . . suddenly comes to feel the mighty power of nature, when one looks it right in the eyes." Her ardor for hunting cooled over the years, however, until she only occasionally shot game for the farm. "It became to me an unreasonable thing . . . for the sake of a few hours' excitement to put out a life that belonged in the great landscape. . . ."* (Shadows on the Grass)

One safari that Tanne was especially fond of recalling occurred during the First World War, when, for lack of a responsible leader, she herself accompanied an ox-caravan bringing supplies to British forces in southern Kenya. (This was actually a series of short trips rather than the long journey she recounts in Out of Africa, *but a marvelous tale nonetheless.) "It was the time when," Judith Thurman observes, "she felt most keenly, without distraction, one with Africa."*

I'M SENDING this letter to you because you are the one person at home who will best understand the exhilaration that comes with the experiences that I am going to describe. I have spent four weeks in the happy hunting grounds and have just emerged from the depths of the great wide open spaces, from the life of prehistoric times, today just as it was a thousand years ago, from meeting with the great beasts of prey, which enthrall one, which obsess one so that one feels that lions are all that one lives for—strengthened by the air of the high mountain region, tanned by its sun, filled with its wild, free, magnificent beauty in heat-dazzling days, in great clear moonlit nights.

[TO INGEBORG DINESEN]

. . . [T]here is something about safari life that makes you forget all your sorrows and feel the whole time as if you had drunk half a bottle of champagne,—bubbling over with heartfelt gratitude for being alive. It seems right that human beings should live in the nomad fashion and unnatural to have one's home always in the same place; one only feels really free when one can go in whatever direction one pleases over the plains, get to the river at sundown and pitch one's camp, with the knowledge that one can fall asleep beneath other trees, with another view before one, the next night. I had not sat by a camp fire for three years, and so sitting there again listening to the lions far out in the darkness was like returning to the really true world again, —where I probably once lived 10,000 years ago. . . .

OUT ON THE Safaris, I had seen a herd of Buffalo, one hundred and twenty-nine of them, come out of the morning mist under a copper sky, one by one, as if the dark and massive, iron-like animals with the mighty horizontally swung horns were not approaching, but were being created before my eyes and sent out as they were finished.

. . . I had seen a herd of Elephant travelling through dense Native forest, where the sunlight is strewn down between the thick creepers in small spots and patches, pacing along as if they had an appointment at the end of the world. It was, in giant size, the border of a very old, infinitely precious Persian carpet, in the dyes of green, yellow and black–brown.

. . . I had time after time watched the progression across the plain of the Giraffe, in their queer, inimitable, vegetative gracefulness, as if it were not a herd of animals but a family of rare, long-stemmed, speckled gigantic flowers slowly advancing.

. . . I had followed two Rhinos on their morning promenade, when they were sniffing and snorting in the air of the dawn,—which is so cold that it hurts in the nose,—and looked like two very big angular stones rollicking in the long valley and enjoying life together. I had seen the royal lion, before sunrise, below a waning moon, crossing the grey plain on his way home from the kill, drawing a dark wake in the silvery grass, his face still red up to the ears, or during the mid-day-siesta, when he reposed contentedly in the midst of his family on the short grass and in the delicate, spring-like shade of the broad Acacia trees of his park of Africa.

THE STELLAR HEAVEN of the Equator is richer than that of the North, and you see it more because you are out more at night. In Northern Europe, winter nights are too cold to allow one much pleasure in the contemplation of the stars, and in summer one hardly distinguishes them within the clear night sky, that is as pale as a dog violet.

The tropical night has the companionability of a Roman Catholic Cathedral compared to the Protestant Churches of the North, which let you in on business only. Here in the great room everybody comes and goes, this is the place where things are going on. To Arabia and Africa, where the sun of the midday kills you, night is the time for travelling and enterprise. The stars have been named here, they have been guides to human beings for many centuries, drawing them in long lines across the desert-sands and the Sea, one towards the East, and another to the West, or the North and South. Cars run well at night, and it is pleasant to motor under the stars, you get into the habit of fixing visits to friends up-country by the time of the next full moon. You start Safaris by the new moon, to have the benefit of the whole row of moonlight nights. It is then strange, when back on a visit to Europe, to find your friends of the towns living out of touch with the moves of the moon and almost in ignorance of them.

I N THE EARLY morning, while the old con-
stellations of the stars were still out, we set
off down the long endless Kijabe Hill, with
the great plains of the Masai Reserve,—iron-
grey in the faint light of the dawn,—spread at
our feet, with lamps tied under the waggons,
swinging, and with much shouting and
cracking of whips. I had four waggons, with
a full team of sixteen oxen to each, and five
spare oxen, and with me twenty-one young
Kikuyus and three Somalis: Farah, Ismail, the
gun-bearer, and an old cook also named
Ismail, a very noble old man. My dog Dusk
walked by my side.

I was out then for three months. When we came down to our place
of destination, we were sent off again to collect the stores of a big
American shooting Safari that had been camping near the border, and
had left in a hurry at the news of the war. From there the waggons
had to go to new places. I learned to know the fords and water-holes
of the Masai Reserve, and to speak a little Masai. The roads everywhere were unbelievably bad, deep with dust, and barred with blocks
of stone taller than the waggons; later we travelled mostly across the
plains. The air of the African highlands went to my head like wine, I
was all the time slightly drunk with it, and the joy of these months
was indescribable.

H OW BEAUTIFUL were the evenings of the Masai reserve when after sunset we arrived at the river or the water-hole where we were to outspan, travelling in a long file. The plains with the thorn-trees on them were already quite dark, but the air was filled with clarity,—and over our heads, to the West, a single star which was to grow big and radiant in the course of the night was now just visible, like a silver point in the sky of citrine topaz. The air was cold to the lungs, the long grass dripping wet, and the herbs on it gave out their spiced astringent scent. In a little while on all sides the Cicada would begin to sing. The grass was me, and the air, the distant invisible mountains were me, the tired oxen were me. I breathed with the slight night-wind in the thorntrees.

. . . This Safari lived for a long time in the memory of the farm. Later on I had many other Safaris, but for some reason,—either because we had at the time been in the service of the Government, a sort of Official ourselves, or because of the war-like atmosphere about it,—this particular expedition was dear to the hearts of the people who had been on it.

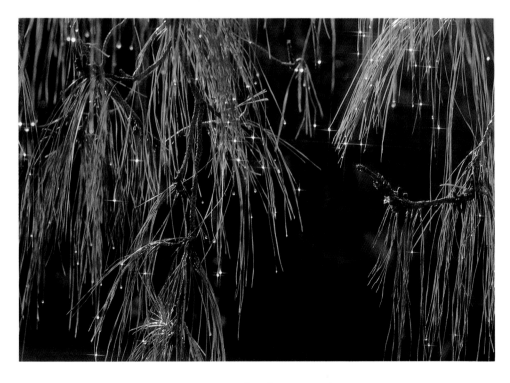

WHEN I WAS down in the Masai Reserve, doing transport for the Government, I one day saw a strange thing, such as no one I know has ever seen. . . . We were walking along in this burning live air, and I was, against my habit, a long way in front of the waggons, with Farah, my dog Dusk and the Toto who looked after Dusk. We were silent, for it was too hot to talk. All at once the plain at the horizon began to move and gallop with more than the atmosphere, a big herd of game was bearing down upon us from the right, diagonally across the stage.

I said to Farah: "Look at all these Wildebeests." But a little after, I was not sure that they were Wildebeests; I took up my field-glasses and looked at them, but that too is difficult in the middle of the day. "Are they Wildebeests, Farah, do you think?" I asked him.

It is very difficult to judge distances on the plains. The quivering air and the monotony of the scenery make it so, also the character of the scattered thorn-trees, which have the exact shape of mighty old forest trees, but are in reality only twelve feet high, so that the Giraffes raise their heads and necks above them. You are continually deceived as to the size of the game that you see at a distance and may, in the middle of the day, mistake a jackal for an Eland, and an ostrich for a Buffalo. A minute later Farah said: "Memsahib, these are wild dogs."

The wild dogs are generally seen three or four at a time, but it happens that you meet a dozen of them together.
. . . They are about the size of a big Alsatian dog. They are black, with a white tuft at the tip of the tail and of the pointed ears.
. . . Here there must have been five hundred wild dogs. They came along in a slow canter, in the strangest way, looking neither right nor left, as if they had been frightened by something, or as if they were travelling fast with a fixed purpose on a track. They just swerved a bit as they came nearer to us; all the same they hardly seemed to see us, and went on at the same pace. When they were closest to us, they were fifty yards away. They were running in a long file, two or three or four side by side, it took time before the whole procession had passed us. In the middle of it, Farah said: "These dogs are very tired, they have run a long way."

WE HAD THE black and white storks in Africa, the birds that build their nests upon the thatched village roofs of Northern Europe. They look less imposing in Africa than they do there, for here they had such tall and ponderous birds as the Marabout and the Secretary Bird to be compared to. The storks have got other habits in Africa than in Europe, where they live as in married couples and are symbols of domestic happiness. Here they are seen together in big flights, as in clubs. They are called locust-birds in Africa, and follow along when the locusts come upon the land, living high on them. They fly over the plains, too, where there is a grass-fire on, circling just in front of the advancing line of small leaping flames, high up in the scintillating rainbow-coloured air, and the grey smoke, on watch for the mice and snakes that run from the fire. The storks have a gay time in Africa.

The Crested Cranes, which come on to the newly rolled and planted maize-land, to steal the maize out of the ground, make up for the robbery by being birds of good omen, announcing the rain; and also by dancing to us. When the tall birds are together in large numbers, it is a fine sight to see them spread their wings and dance.

The Greater Hornbill was another visitor to the farm, and came there to eat the fruits of the Cape-Chestnut tree. They are very strange birds. It is an adventure or an experience to meet them, not altogether pleasant, for they look exceedingly knowing. One morning before sunrise I was woken up by a loud jabbering outside the house, and when I walked out on the terrace I saw forty-one Hornbills sitting in the trees on the lawn. There they looked less like birds than like some fantastic articles of finery set on the trees here and there by a child.

A LION ON THE PLAIN bears a greater likeness to ancient monumental stone lions than to the lion which to-day you see in a zoo; the sight of him goes straight to the heart. Dante cannot have been more deeply amazed and moved at the first sight of Beatrice in a street of Florence. Gazing back into the past I do, I believe, remember each individual lion I have seen—his coming into the picture, his slow raising or rapid turning of the head, the strange, snakelike swaying of his tail. "Praise be to thee, Lord, for Brother Lion, the which is very calm, with mighty paws, and flows through the flowing grass, red-mouthed, silent, with the roar of the thunder ready in his chest."

THE ELEPHANT, which through centuries has been the one head of game hunted for profit, in the course of time has adopted man into his scheme of things, with deep distrust. Our nearness to him is a challenge which he will never disregard; he comes towards us, straightly and quickly, on his own, a towering, overwhelming structure, massive as cast iron and lithe as running water.

. . . In very old days the elephant, upon the roof of the earth, led an existence deeply satisfying to himself and fit to be set up as an example to the rest of creation: that of a being mighty and powerful beyond anyone's attack, attacking no one. The grandiose and idyllic modus vivendi lasted till an old Chinese painter had his eyes opened to the sublimity of ivory as a background to his paintings, or a young dancer of Zanzibar hers to the beauty of an ivory anklet. Then they began to appear to all sides of him, small alarming figures in the landscape drawing closer: the Wanderobo with his poisoned arrows, the Arab ivory-hunter with his long silver-mounted muzzle-loader, and the white professional elephant-killer with his heavy rifle. The manifestation of the glory of God was turned into an object of exploitation. Is it to be wondered at that he cannot forgive us?

Yet there is always something magnanimous about elephants. To follow a rhino in his own country is hard work; the space that he clears in the thorn-thicket is just a few inches too low for the hunter, and he will have to keep his head bent a little all the time. The elephant on his march through dense forest calmly tramples out a green fragrant tunnel, lofty like the nave of a cathedral. . . . There is a morally edifying quality as well in the very aspect of an elephant—on seeing four elephants walking together on the plain, I at once felt that I had been shown black stone sculptures of the four major Prophets.

BERKELEY COLE and I, in a private jargon of ours, distinguished between respectability and decency, and divided up our acquaintances, human and animal, in accordance with the doctrine. We put down domestic animals as respectable and wild animals as decent, and held that, while the existence and prestige of the first were decided by their relation to the community, the others stood in direct contact with God. Pigs and poultry, we agreed, were worthy of our respect, inasmuch as they loyally returned what was invested in them, and in their most intimate private life behaved as was expected of them. We watched them in their sties and yards, perseveringly working at the return of investments made, pleasantly feeding, grunting and quacking. And leaving them there, to their own homely, cosy atmosphere, we turned our eyes to the unrespectable, destructive wild boar on his lonely wanderings, or to those unrespectable, shameless corn-thieves, the wild geese and duck, in their purposeful line of flight across the sky, and we felt their course to have been drawn up by the finger of God.

We registered ourselves with the wild animals, sadly admitting the inadequacy of our return to the community—and to our mortgages—but realizing that we could not possibly, not even in order to obtain the highest approval of our surroundings, give up that direct contact with God which we shared with the hippo and the flamingo. Nine thousand feet up we felt safe, and we laughed at the ambition of the new arrivals, of the Missions, the business people and the Government itself, to make the continent of Africa respectable.

PART FIVE

Flight and Fall

[EDITOR'S NOTE]

Karen Blixen's last years in Africa encompassed the most intense joys and the most profound tragedies of her life. In 1918, while still married to Bror, she had met Denys Finch Hatton, the younger son of the Earl of Winchelsea, "a tall, witty, lean, wry, balding, impossibly handsome aristocrat" (Judith Thurman), who had come out to Africa several years before the Blixens and who occupied his nomadic spirit with trading, safaris, and piloting small planes (for British forces in Egypt and later on his private business). Their relationship, described with reticence in Out of Africa *but more frankly in her letters, was certainly the love of Tanne's life. Though he lived in her house in the interludes between his travels, they never married—chiefly because Denys's great physical and mental attractiveness, which had made him since childhood the object of adoration by family and friends, also made him "terrified of being bored, depended upon, exploited, or possessed."*

*If Denys never offered the security that Karen's emotional life so lacked, he did provide her with "the most transporting pleasure of my life on the farm"—flying with him over the Ngong Hills and more distant parts of Kenya. "There, where there are few or no roads and where you can land on the plains, flying becomes a thing of real and vital importance in your life, it opens up a world." (*Out of Africa*) Judith Thurman suggests that these flights fulfilled another need in Tanne, that of attaining some distance or perspective on the disasters that were soon to overwhelm her and bring her life in Africa to an end.*

The Ngong farm had always been financially marginal, requiring frequent large infusions of capital from her family and other stockholders in the Karen Coffee Company. Family members—including Tanne's brother Thomas Dinesen; her mother, Ingeborg; and her uncle Aage Westenholz—from time to time visited the farm, their purpose at least in part to investigate its economy, and on her visits home to Denmark Tanne spent much time pleading her cause to them. Finally she lost the battle: unfavorable conditions, poor management, and years of bad harvests resulted, in December 1930, in the forced sale of the farm at auction. Tanne had five months to harvest her last crop and settle her affairs in Kenya.

*Another great blow followed shortly. In May 1931, Denys's plane crashed on take-off from Voi, in Tanganyika, killing him and a servant named Kamau. Although he and Tanne had recently quarreled and he no longer lived at Ngong, she arranged to have him buried in the hills near the farm, at a spot they had once picked out for their graves. Much later she would write, "Fate had willed it that my visitors to the farm by that time [soon after her return to Denmark] had already gone. . . . There they were, all of them, nine thousand feet up, safe in the mould of Africa, slowly being turned into African mould themselves. And here was I, walking in the fair woods of Denmark. . . ." (*Shadows on the Grass*)*

In late July of 1931, Karen Blixen embarked from Mombasa to Marseilles, leaving Africa for the last time.

ON THE WESTERN WALL of my house there was a stone seat and in front of it a table made out of a mill-stone. This stone had a tragic history: it was the upper mill-stone of the mill of the two murdered Indians. After the murder nobody dared to take over the mill, it was empty and silent for a long time, and I had the stone brought up to my house to form a table top, to remind me of Denmark. The Indian millers had told me that their mill-stone had come over the Sea from Bombay, as the stones of Africa are not hard enough for the work of grinding. On the top side a pattern was carved, and it had a few large brown spots on it, which my house-boys held to be the blood of the Indians, that would never come off. The mill-stone table in a way constituted the centre of the farm, for I used to sit behind it in all my dealings with the Natives. From the stone seat behind the mill-stone, I and Denys Finch-Hatton had one New Year seen the new moon and the planets of Venus and Jupiter all close together, in a group on the sky; it was such a radiant sight that you could hardly believe it to be real, and I have never seen it again.

Denys Finch-Hatton had no other home in Africa than the farm, he lived in my house between his Safaris, and kept his books and his gramophone there. When he came back to the farm, it gave out what was in it; it spoke,—as the coffee-plantations speak, when with the first showers of the rainy season they flower, dripping wet, a cloud of chalk. When I was expecting Denys back, and heard his car coming up the drive, I heard, at the same time, the things of the farm all telling what they really were.

To DENYS Finch-Hatton I owe what was, I think, the greatest, the most transporting pleasure of my life on the farm: I flew with him over Africa. There, where there are few or no roads and where you can land on the plains, flying becomes a thing of real and vital importance in your life, it opens up a world. Denys had brought out his Moth machine; it could land on my plain on the farm only a few minutes from the house, and we were up nearly every day.

. . . Where you are sitting in front of your pilot, with nothing but space before you, you feel that he is carrying you upon the out-stretched palms of his hands, as the Djinn carried Prince Ali through the air, and that the wings that bear you onward are his.

. . . You have tremendous views as you get up above the African highlands, surprising combinations and changes of light and colour-ing, the rainbow on the green sunlit land, the gigantic upright clouds and big wild black storms, all swing round you in a race and a dance. The lashing hard showers of rain whiten the air askance. The lan-guage is short of words for the experiences of flying, and will have to invent new words with time. When you have flown over the Rift Valley and the volcanoes of Suswa and Longonot, you have travelled far and have been to the lands on the other side of the moon. You may at other times fly low enough to see the animals on the plains and to feel towards them as God did when he had just created them, and before he commissioned Adam to give them names.

. . . Every time that I have gone up in an aeroplane and looking down have realised that I was free of the ground, I have had the consciousness of a great new discovery. "I see:" I have thought, "This was the idea. And now I understand everything."

ONE DAY Denys and I flew to Lake Natron, ninety miles South-East of the farm, and more than four thousand feet lower, two thousand feet above Sea level. Lake Natron is the place from where they take soda. The bottom of the lake and the shores are like some sort of whitish concrete, with a strong, sour and salt smell.

The sky was blue, but as we flew from the plains in over the stony and bare lower country, all colour seemed to be scorched out of it. The whole landscape below us looked like delicately marked tortoise-shell. Suddenly, in the midst of it was the lake. The white bottom, shining through the water, gives it, when seen from the air, a striking, an unbelievable azure-colour, so clear that for a moment you shut your eyes at it; the expanse of water lies in the bleak tawny land like a big bright aquamarine.

We had been flying high, now we went down, and as we sank our
own shade, dark-blue, floated under us upon the light-blue lake.
Here live thousands of Flamingoes, although I do not know how they
exist in the brackish water,—surely there are no fish here. At our
approach they spread out in large circles and fans, like the rays of a
setting sun, like an artful Chinese pattern on silk or porcelain, form-
ing itself and changing, as we looked at it.

WHEN DENYS AND I had not time for long journeys we went out for a short flight over the Ngong Hills, generally about sunset. These hills, which are amongst the most beautiful in the world, are perhaps at their loveliest seen from the air, when the ridges, bare towards the four peaks, mount, and run side by side with the aeroplane, or suddenly sink down and flatten out into a small lawn.

Here in the hills there were Buffaloes. I had even, in my very young days,—when I could not live till I had killed a specimen of each kind of African game,—shot a bull out here. Later on, when I was not so keen to shoot as to watch the wild animals, I had been out to see them again. I had camped in the hills by a spring half way to the top, bringing my servants, tents, and provisions with me, and Farah and I had been up in the dark, ice cold mornings to creep and crawl through bush and long grass, in the hope of catching a glimpse of the herd; but twice I had had to go back without success. That the herd lived there, neighbours of mine to the West, was still a value in the life on the farm, but they were serious-minded, self-sufficient neighbours, the old nobility of the hills, now somehow reduced; they did not receive much.

In the Ngong Hills there also lived a pair of eagles. Denys in the afternoons used to say: "Let us go and visit the eagles." I have once seen one of them sitting on a stone near the top of the mountain, and getting up from it, but otherwise they spent their life up in the air. Many times we have chased one of these eagles, careening and throwing ourselves on to one wing and then to the other, and I believe that the sharp-sighted bird played with us. Once, when we were running side by side, Denys stopped his engine in mid air, and as he did so I heard the eagle screech.

Denys owned a piece of land down at the coast, thirty miles North of Mombasa on the Creek of Takaunga. Here were the ruins of an old Arab settlement, with a very modest minaret and a well,—a weathered growth of grey stone on the salted soil, and in the midst of it a few old Mango trees. He had built a small house on his land and I had stayed there. The scenery was of a divine, clean, barren Marine greatness, with the blue Indian Ocean before you, the deep creek of Takaunga to the South, and the long steep unbroken coast-line of pale grey and yellow coral-rock as far as the eye reached.

It was full moon while I was down at Takaunga, and the beauty of the
radiant, still nights was so perfect that the heart bent under it. You
slept with the doors open to the silver Sea; the playing warm breeze
in a low whisper swept in a little loose sand, on to the stone floor.
One night a row of Arab dhows came along, close to the coast, running noiselessly before the monsoon, a file of brown shadow-sails
under the moon.

Denys sometimes talked of making Takaunga his home in Africa, and of starting his Safaris from there. When I began to talk of
having to leave the farm, he offered me his house down there, as he
had had mine in the highlands.

[TO ANDERS DINESEN]

Merry Christmas, and very best wishes for a really happy 1928.
You know, we clodhoppers understand each other and must stick
together,—if only the good God had a sense of liberty, equality, and
fraternity and could have let me have a bit of your downpour in 1927;
you would have been heartily welcome to some of my drought.
. . . I am busy getting off the trees what coffee I can that has not dried
up and fallen off already, and think I will not do too badly after all;
but it is heartrending to see the bushes covered with little dry, black
berries after being lovely white blossom in the spring and which
could have grown into big red coffee berries at £140 a ton, if the
heavens had not been so utterly contrary.

. . . I know quite well that Karen Coffee Co. have got the idea into
their heads that they are going to be bankrupted, but no such thing as
that is going to happen. And here there are miles of unrestricted
plains, green marshes and fine thorn forests, huge flocks of zebra and
wildebeest gallop along, elephants stroll and lions roar for you and
your peers, but no one knows how long it will last; for there are not
so many places left in the world where nature is still undisturbed and
that have not been marked by the hand of man.

[130]

WHEN I HAD no more money, and could not make things pay, I had to sell the farm. A big Company in Nairobi bought it. They thought that the place was too high up for coffee, and they were not going in for farming. But they meant to take up all the coffee-trees, to divide up the land and lay out roads, and in time, when Nairobi should be growing out to the West, they meant to sell the land for building-plots.

The people of the farm who grieved most at my departure were I think the old women. The old Kikuyu women have had a hard life, and have themselves become flint-hard under it, like old mules which will bite you if they can come to it. They were more difficult for any disease to kill off than their men, as I learned in my practice as a doctor, and they were wilder than the men, and, even more thoroughly than they, devoid of the faculty of admiration. They had borne a number of children and had seen many of them die; they were afraid of nothing. They carried loads of firewood,—with a rein round their foreheads to steady them,—of three hundred pounds, tottering below them, but unsubdued; they worked in the hard ground of their shambas, standing on their heads from the early morning till late in the evening. . . . And they had a stock of energy in them still; they radiated vitality. . . . This strength, and love of life in them, to me seemed not only highly respectable, but glorious and bewitching.

THERE WAS A PLACE in the Hills, on the first ridge in the Game Reserve, that I myself at the time when I thought that I was to live and die in Africa, had pointed out to Denys as my future burial-place. In the evening, while we sat and looked at the hills, from my house, he remarked that then he would like to be buried there himself as well. Since then, sometimes when we drove out in the hills, Denys had said: "Let us drive as far as our graves." Once when we were camped in the hills to look for Buffalo, we had in the afternoon walked over to the slope to have a closer look at it. There was an infinitely great view from there; in the light of the sunset we saw both Mount Kenya and Kilimanjaro. Denys had been eating an orange, lying in the grass, and had said he would like to stay there.

. . . Here in the early afternoon they brought out Denys from Nairobi, following his old Safari-track to Tanganyika, and driving slowly on the wet road. When they came to the last steep slope, they lifted out, and carried the narrow coffin, that was covered with the flag. As it was placed in the grave, the country changed and became the setting for it, as still as itself, the hills stood up gravely, they knew and understood what we were doing in them; after a little while they themselves took charge of the ceremony, it was an action between them and him, and the people present became a party of very small lookers-on in the landscape.

Denys had watched and followed all the ways of the African Highlands, and better than any other white man, he had known their soil and seasons, the vegetation and the wild animals, the winds and smells. He had observed the changes of weather in them, their people, clouds, the stars at night. Here in the hills, I had seen him only a short time ago, standing bare-headed in the afternoon sun, gazing out over the land, and lifting his field-glasses to find out everything about it. He had taken in the country, and in his eyes and his mind it had been changed, marked by his own individuality, and made part of him. Now Africa received him, and would change him, and make him one with herself.

I often drove out to Denys's grave. In a bee-line, it was not more than five miles from my house, but round by the road it was fifteen. The grave was a thousand feet higher up than my house, the air was different here, as clear as a glass of water; light sweet winds lifted your hair when you took off your hat; over the peaks of the hills, the clouds came wandering from the East, drew their live shadow over the wide undulating land, and were dissolved and disappeared over the Rift Valley.

IN THE HARBOUR of Mombasa lay a rusty German cargo-steamer, homeward bound. Upon the deck there stood a tall wooden case, and above the edge of the case rose the heads of two Giraffes. They were, Farah, who had been on board the boat, told me, coming from Portuguese East Africa, and were going to Hamburg, to a travelling Menagerie.

The Giraffes turned their delicate heads from the one side to the other, as if they were surprised, which they might well be. They had not seen the Sea before. They could only just have room to stand in the narrow case. The world had suddenly shrunk, changed and closed round them.

They could not know or imagine the degradation to which they were sailing. For they were proud and innocent creatures, gentle amblers of the great plains; they had not the least knowledge of captivity, cold, stench, smoke, and mange, nor of the terrible boredom in a world in which nothing is ever happening.

. . . In the long years before them, will the Giraffes sometimes dream of their lost country? Where are they now, where have they gone to, the grass and the thorn-trees, the rivers and water-holes and the blue mountains? The high sweet air over the plains has lifted and withdrawn. Where have the other Giraffes gone to, that were side by side with them when they set going, and cantered over the undulating land? They have left them, they have all gone, and it seems that they are never coming back.

In the night where is the full moon?

W HEN I LOOK BACK upon my last months in Africa, it seems to me that the lifeless things were aware of my departure a long time before I was so myself. The hills, the forests, plains and rivers, the wind, all knew that we were to part. When I first began to make terms with fate, and the negotiations about the sale of the farm were taken up, the attitude of the landscape towards me changed. Till then I had been part of it, and the drought had been to me like a fever, and the flowering of the plain like a new frock. Now the country disengaged itself from me, and stood back a little, in order that I should see it clearly and as a whole.

The hills can do the same thing in the week before the rains. On an evening as you look at them, they suddenly make a great movement and uncover, they become as manifest, as distinct and vivid in form and colour, as if they meant to yield themselves to you, with all that they contain, as if you could walk from where you sit, on to the green slope. . . . In the hills, in March, this gesture of abandon means that the rains are near, but here, to me, it meant parting.

I said good-bye to each of my house-boys, and, as I went out, they, who had been carefully instructed to close the doors, left the door wide open behind me. This was a typical Native gesture, as if they meant that I was to come back again, or else they did so to emphasize that there was now nothing more to close the doors of the house on, and they might as well be open to all the winds. Farah was driving me, slowly, at the pace of a riding-camel I suppose, round by the drive and out of sight of the house.

. . . At the Samburu station on the line, I got out of the train while the engine was taking in water, and walked with Farah on the platform.

From there, to the South-West, I saw the Ngong Hills. The noble wave of the mountain rose above the surrounding flat land, all air-blue. But it was so far away that the four peaks looked trifling, hardly distinguishable, and different from the way they looked from the farm. The outline of the mountain was slowly smoothed and levelled out by the hand of distance.

AFTER I HAD LEFT Africa, Gustav Mohr wrote to me of a strange thing that had happened by Denys's grave, the like of which I have never heard. "The Masai," he wrote, "have reported to the District Commissioner at Ngong, that many times, at sunrise and sunset, they have seen lions on Finch-Hatton's grave in the Hills. A lion and a lioness have come there, and stood, or lain, on the grave for a long time. Some of the Indians who have passed the place in their lorries on the way to Kajado have also seen them. After you went away, the ground round the grave was levelled out, into a sort of big terrace, I suppose that the level place makes a good site for the lions, from there they can have a view over the plain, and the cattle and game on it."

[A Note on the Sources]

Passages excerpted from *Out of Africa* appear in this book on pages 4, 5, 6, 9, 10, 11, 12, 13, 14, 19, 20, 28, 30, 32, 36, 40, 41, 42, 43, 44, 45, 46, 47, 48, 49, 50, 51, 52, 56, 57, 58, 59, 61, 66, 68, 69, 70, 71, 72, 73, 74, 75, 77, 80, 81, 83, 84, 85, 89, 96, 97, 98, 99, 100, 103, 104, 105, 106, 107, 108, 109, 120, 121, 122, 124, 125, 126, 128, 129, 131, 132, 133, 135, 136, 137, 139.

Passages from *Shadows on the Grass* appear on pages 78, 79, 82, 86, 87, 110, 112, 113, 114.

Excerpts from *Letters from Africa: 1914–1931* are headed by the recipient's name, and can be so identified.

Works by Isak Dinesen about Africa

Out of Africa. London: Putnam, 1937; New York: Random House, 1938.

> The most readily available edition of *Out of Africa* is the Vintage Books paperback edition, first published in 1972. As of late 1985, a new Vintage paperback will be available, incorporating *Out of Africa* and *Shadows on the Grass* in one volume.

Shadows on the Grass, New York: Random House; London: Michael Joseph, 1961.

> Also most readily available in the Vintage Books paperback edition (1974); and see the note above.

Letters from Africa: 1914–1931. Edited by Frans Lasson. Translated by Anne Born. Chicago and London: University of Chicago Press, 1981.

> Frans Lasson's chronology of Isak Dinesen's life, included in *Letters from Africa*, was a most helpful reference.

Other Sources

Beard, Peter, ed. *Longing for Darkness: Kamante's Tales from Out of Africa*. New York: Harcourt Brace Jovanovich, 1975.

> A remarkable compilation of Kamante's stories as told to and transcribed by Peter Beard, with photographs and drawings; out of print and difficult to obtain.

Lasson, Frans, and Svendsen, Clara, eds. *The Life and Destiny of Isak Dinesen*. New York: Random House, 1970; Chicago and London: University of Chicago Press, 1976.

> A pictorial history of Dinesen's life; the Phoenix paperback edition published by Chicago remains in print.

Thurman, Judith. *Isak Dinesen: The Life of a Storyteller*. New York: St. Martin's Press, 1982.

> Thurman's definitive life won the 1983 American Book Award for biography, and is available in paperback.

Trzebinski, Errol. *Silence Will Speak*. London: Heinemann, 1977; Chicago: University of Chicago Press, 1978.

> The only biography to date of Denys Finch Hatton. Out of print in hardcover, but a paperback edition is scheduled for late 1985 release by the University of Chicago Press.

[ABOUT THE PHOTOGRAPHS]

NOTE: The photographers of some of the historical photographs of Isak Dinesen's life in African remain unidentified.

Page i Acacia at sunrise, Serengeti National Park, Tanzania. By Galen Rowell.

Page ii Karen Blixen and her deerhounds. Courtesy of the Rungstedlund Foundation.

Page vi Karen Blixen at her coffee factory. By Thomas Dinesen / Courtesy of Peter Beard.

Page xviii Giraffes, Arusha National Park, Tanzania. By Galen Rowell.

Page 3 Karen Blixen with her dog Dusk in the Ngong Hills. Courtesy of the Rungstedlund Foundation.

Page 4 Baobabs and acacias, Tarangire National Park, Tanzania. By Bill O'Connor / Peter Arnold, Inc.

Page 5 Thornbush at sunset. By Leonard Lee Rue III / Earth Scenes.

Pages 6-7 Masai Mara Game Reserve. By Michael and Barbara Reed / Earth Scenes.

Page 8 Diani Beach, Kenya coast. By Henry Ausloos / Earth Scenes.

Page 9 Ruins of Shela, Lamu Island. By Jack Couffer / Bruce Coleman, Inc.

Page 10 Sheik Sudani Mosque, Mombasa. By J. C. Carton / Bruce Coleman, Inc.

Page 11 Young elephant at dawn, Masai Mara. By Yann Arthus-Bertrand / Peter Arnold, Inc.

Page 13 Mombasa harbor. By Bill Ruth / Bruce Coleman, Inc.

Page 14 Fort Jesus, Mombasa. By J. C. Carton / Bruce Coleman, Inc.

Page 15 *Top:* Street scene, Lamu Town, Kenya coast. By J. C. Carton / Bruce Coleman, Inc. *Bottom:* Market, Mombasa. By C. Henneghien / Bruce Coleman, Inc.

Page 16 Muthaiga Country Club, Nairobi. Courtesy of Peter Beard.

Page 17 Wildebeest and zebra, Masai Mara. By Galen Rowell.

Page 19 *Top:* Farmland, central highlands. By Audrey Ross / Bruce Coleman, Inc. *Bottom:* The Blixens arrive at Mbagathi. By Frank Connors / © 1985 by Universal City Studios, Inc.

Page 20 Nairobi in the 1920s. Courtesy of Peter Beard.

Page 21 *Top:* Government House, Nairobi. *Bottom:* Ox-drawn water cart, Nairobi. Both courtesy of Peter Beard.

Pages 22-23 Elephant and wildebeest, Tarangire National Park, Tanzania. By Galen Rowell.

Page 24 Small farming plots, central highlands. By Bill Ruth / Bruce Coleman, Inc.

Page 27 Mbogani House. By Thomas Dinesen / Courtesy of the Rungstedlund Foundation.

Page 29 Kikuyu farms and Mount Kenya. By Norman Myers / Bruce Coleman, Inc.

Page 31 Giraffes, Tsavo National Park. By Patti Murray / Animals Animals.

Page 32 *Top:* Chyulu Hills. By Delta Willis / Bruce Coleman, Inc. *Bottom:* Alpine flora on Mount Kenya. By A. J. Deane / Bruce Coleman, Inc.

Page 33 Giant groundsel on Mount Kenya. By Galen Rowell.

Page 34 Karen Blixen and Mbogani House, 1922. Courtesy of Peter Beard.

Page 35 *Top left:* Reichenow's weaver, near Nairobi. By Galen Rowell. *Top right:* Superb starling. By Steven C. Kaufman / Peter Arnold, Inc. *Bottom:* Waxbill, near Nairobi. By Galen Rowell.

Page 37 *Top:* Black rhinoceros. By Douglas Kirkland / © 1985 by Universal Pictures, Inc. *Bottom left:* Eland, Ngorongoro Crater, Tanzania. By Galen Rowell. *Bottom right:* Old bull buffalo. By Yann Arthus-Bertrand / Peter Arnold, Inc.

Pages 38-39 The Rift Valley. By Peter Davey / Bruce Coleman, Inc.

Page 40 Pyrethrum farm, central highlands. By M. Philip Kahl / Bruce Coleman, Inc.

Page 41 Planting coffee. By Frank Connors / © 1985 by Universal City Studios, Inc.

Page 42 Cattle drink from pond near the dam Karen Blixen had built. By Thomas Dinesen / Courtesy of the Rungstedlund Foundation.

Page 43 *Top:* Impala at waterhole, Isiolo–Samburu Game Reserve. By David C. Fritts. *Bottom:* White-necked cormorants, Lake Manyara, Tanzania. By Galen Rowell.

Page 44 Wildflower, Arusha National Park, Tanzania. By Galen Rowell.

Page 45 Rainforest on Mount Kenya. By David C. Fritts.

Page 46 *Top:* Black-faced vervet, Arusha National Park. *Bottom:* Warthog, Arusha National Park. Both by Galen Rowell.

Page 47 Waterfall, Aberdare Mountains. By M. Philip Kahl / Bruce Coleman, Inc.

Page 48 Karen Blixen feeding the adopted bushbuck fawn, Lulu. Courtesy of the Rungstedlund Foundation.

Page 49 *Top:* Bushbuck doe. *Bottom:* Male bushbuck. Both by Peter Davey / Bruce Coleman, Inc.

Page 50 Storm over the Masai Mara. By Peter Davey / Bruce Coleman, Inc.